THE LIVES AND EXPLOITS

HIGHWAYMEN, ROGUES, *AND* MURDERERS

Dedicated to Ernest, Audrey & Benjamin Trundley

(Whether they would have approved of having their names attached to a book containing the life stories notorious thieves, murderers, scoundrels, and reprobates – well, I'm not too sure...)

THE LIVES AND EXPLOITS OF THE MOST NOTED

HIGHWAYMEN, ROGUES, AND MURDERERS

STEPHEN BASDEO

PEN & SWORD
HISTORY

First published in Great Britain in 2018 by
PEN AND SWORD HISTORY
an imprint of
Pen and Sword Books Ltd
47 Church Street
Barnsley
South Yorkshire S70 2AS

ISBN 978 1 52671 316 2

Printed and bound in the UK by TJ International Ltd,
Padstow, Cornwall

Typeset in Times New Roman 11/13.5 by
Aura Technology and Software Services, India

Pen & Sword Books Ltd incorporates the imprints of Pen & Sword
Archaeology, Atlas, Aviation, Battleground, Discovery,
Family History, History, Maritime, Military, Naval, Politics, Railways,
Select, Social History, Transport, True Crime, Claymore Press,
Frontline Books, Leo Cooper, Praetorian Press, Remember When,
Seaforth Publishing and Wharncliffe.

For a complete list of Pen and Sword titles please contact
Pen and Sword Books Limited
47 Church Street, Barnsley, South Yorkshire, S70 2AS, England
E-mail: enquiries@pen-and-sword.co.uk
Website: www.pen-and-sword.co.uk

Contents

****

To the READER

Instead of the ERRATA.

This rogue hath had his faults, the printers too;
All men whilst here do erre; and so may you.

****

Errata notice from Richard Head's *The English Rogue* (1665)

Acknowledgements

First off, I would like to thank, as always, my family; my parents, Debbie and Joseph Basdeo, and my sister, Jamila and her family. The emotional support from them that I have received while I was writing this book as well as finishing off my PhD thesis has been invaluable. My friends, Rich, Sam, Chris, and Myk also get a big kiss from me. And of course, my cat, Robin, named after the original and greatest highwayman, Robin Hood.

An additional note of thanks goes to my supervisors, Professor Paul Hardwick, Professor Rosemary Mitchell, and Dr Alaric Hall, of the University of Leeds, for being generally awesome and helping me to develop my skills as a writer. Paul is particularly good at highlighting the fact, in all of my writing, that when I am referring to a historical text I should speak about it in the historic present because the text still physically exists – 'the text says...' instead of 'the text said'. Hopefully, I have not fallen back into this bad habit in this book. Also, Professor Heather Shore from Leeds Beckett deserves many thanks; it was under her guidance and supervision that I completed two crime-related theses while studying for both my BA and MA degrees in history.

Another word of gratitude goes to my friend, Allen Wright, whose *Bold Outlaw* website has been invaluable for everyone interested in researching the legend of Robin Hood, and certainly helped me in drafting a PhD research proposal back in 2014, and whose work has once again been useful for me in writing this book. Finally, the lovely people at Pen and Sword Books who have helped make this book possible: Jonathan Wright (my commissioning editor); Laura Hirst; and Lauren Burton; and of course the design team at P&S who patiently tolerated the numerous amendments I made to the supposedly final manuscript of *Wat Tyler*! And last, but certainly by no means least, my editor, Carol Trow – many thanks!

Preface

Let us the road.
Hark! I hear the sound of coaches!
The hour of attack approaches,
To your arms, brave boys, and load.

See the ball I hold!
Let the chymists toil like asses,
Our fire their fire surpasses,
And turns all our lead to gold.
        John Gay, *The Beggar's Opera* (1728)

'There are few subjects that interest us more generally, than the adventures of robbers and banditti. In our infancy they awaken and rivet our attention as much as the best fairy tales, and when our happy credulity in all things is woefully abated, and our faith in the supernatural fled, we still retain our taste for the adventurous deeds and wild lives of brigands.'
        Charles Macfarlane, *Lives of the Banditti* (1833)

Macfarlane's words generally ring true. In our youth, many of us were entertained with tales of robbers and bandits. Ask people what their favourite Disney movie was when they were growing up and it is likely that some of them will refer to Disney's *Robin Hood* (1973). As people grow older, they may develop an interest in watching films and television shows featuring the suave mobster, or the police procedural which depicts the lives of those who catch criminals. As entertainment, crime sells, and it has been the same since the early modern period. The present work, in fact, is intended as a successor to a popular genre of literature that flourished during the eighteenth century; the criminal biography. In works such as Alexander Smith's *A Complete History of the Lives and Robberies of the Most Notorious Highwaymen* (1719), Charles Johnson's *Lives of the*

Most Remarkable Criminals (1735), *The Newgate Calendar* (1774), and *The Criminal Recorder* (1804), the lives of notorious offenders were sensationalised for an enthusiastic audience hungry to gain a glimpse into the lives of the criminal 'other'. It is from books such as these that people in the eighteenth century gained their understanding of crime and the criminal underworld. Even today, our understanding of notorious criminals and their *modus operandi* is to a large extent shaped by popular culture; their life stories are told in newspapers, magazines, novels, television dramas, and in movies. For many of the medieval and early modern outlaws who are featured in this book, much of what we know of their lives comes not from trial reports, but from ballads and pamphlets printed after their deaths. Before entering into our history of the most notorious highwaymen, let us gain a brief overview of the development of crime literature throughout the centuries, we can see the connections between criminals, public perceptions of crime, and popular culture.

There are few writings pertaining to bandits that have survived from the ancient world, and were it not for the various laws enacted against highway robbers during the period, we would have very little information on these early rogues at all. The Bible (if we lay religious ideology aside momentarily) tells us that banditry and highway robbery was a common feature of life in the ancient world. The only works from Europe during antiquity that enter into any significant detail upon the lives of individual bandits are the writings of Cassius Dio (155–235AD) and Herodian (170–240AD). These men's writings certainly cannot be classed as crime literature as we would understand the genre today, but they do provide a small amount of information on two highway robbers named Bulla Felix and Maternus. Felix's story is included in the appendix because it offers some interesting parallels to medieval and early modern Robin Hood stories.

It is in medieval Europe that we first see the emergence of a popular culture connected to criminals. In an age when there was no organised system of law enforcement and imprisonment, summary justice was the preferred method of punishment for minor offenders and, for graver offences where the offender had not been caught, it was much easier for the authorities to proclaim that a certain offender was an outlaw. The sentence literally placed the offender beyond the protection of the law. This allowed him (and outlaws were usually male) to be pursued and killed on sight by anyone. The most famous medieval outlaws are Earl Godwin (d.1066), Hereward the Wake (c.1035–c.1072), Eustache the Monk (c.1170–1217),

Fouke Fitzwarren (c.1160–1268), the legendary Adam Bell, and of course Robin Hood (twelfth-thirteenth centuries). Tales of Robin Hood circulated orally from at least the fourteenth century, and likely before that as well. The first written reference to stories of an outlaw named Robin Hood appears in the B text of William Langland's *The Vision of Piers Plowman* (c.1377), in which a lazy clergyman named Sloth says, 'I can noughte parfitly my Paternoster as the prest it syngeth, but I can rymes of Robyn Hood, and Randolf Erle of Chestre'.[1] Some manuscript versions of these oral tales survive, and there are four early ballads which all date in their final form to the fifteenth century: *Robin Hood and the Monk*; *Robin Hood and the Potter*; *A Gest of Robyn Hode*; and *Robin Hood's Death*. Of these early tales, the *Gest* is the most significant, although in none of the early ballads does Robin Hood actually steal from the rich to give to the poor. All that is said of Robin's social mission in *A Gest of Robyn Hode* is that there are certain people whom the outlaws must leave alone:

> "'But loke ye do no husbonde harme,
> That tylleth with his plough.
>
> "No more ye shall no good yeman
> That walketh by grene wode shawe,
> Ne no knyght ne no squyer
> That wol be a gode felawe.'"
>
> ["But look you do no husbandman harm,
> That tills with a plough.
>
> "Neither any good yeoman
> That walks in the greenwood shawe,
> Neither any knight or squire,
> That would be a good fellow."][2]

At the end of the poem, it is said that Robin Hood 'dyde pore men moch god'. It would be up to sixteenth century chroniclers to expand upon this theme and cast him as the 'Prince of Thieves' who redistributes his wealth to the destitute. Some scholars also believe that another ballad entitled *Robyn and Gandelyn* relates to Robin Hood, although its place in the Robin Hood tradition has been questioned by some historians.[3] With the arrival of printing, some of the outlaw tales began to be published. Five printed editions of *A Gest of Robyn Hode* survive from the sixteenth century.[4] Six editions of *Adam Bell, Clim of the Clough, and William of Cloudeslie* appeared in the same century, with several more printings occurring in the next century. Clearly, sixteenth century readers wanted to believe in the myth of a good outlaw.

In the same century these ballads were being printed, rogue literature appeared. In this genre, the spaces that criminals are known to inhabit move from the greenwood to the town, and criminals ultimately become more menacing. Works such as Gilbert Walker's *Manifest Detection of Diceplay* (1552), John Awdley's *The Fraternity of Vagabonds* (1561), and Thomas Dekker's *Lantern and Candlelight* (1608) gave contemporary readers a glimpse into the sinister practises of cony-catchers, rogues, vagabonds, and thieves in Tudor and Stuart England. They were meant to titillate respectable readers but also to warn them of the many dastardly schemes that they could fall foul of if they were to visit the capital. These men were not the good outlaws of medieval ballads who wore suits of Lincoln-green and robbed only corrupt clergyman and sheriffs. Rogues and vagabonds in Tudor England would rob from people indiscriminately. In fact, in urban areas even the women were to be feared; the spirit that is sent up from hell in *Lantern and Candlelight* is conned first by a woman who leads him into the back of her shop, and there he is set upon by a gang of rabid young apprentices. The poor devil from hell concludes that the backstreets of London offer more torture for a demon than hell ever could. Designated as 'masterless men' by the authorities, these people were a law unto themselves. They were not easily identifiable as the greenwood outlaws of the past were, but were indistinguishable from the law-abiding. They even had their own secret 'underworld' language. Thus, the works of Awdley, Dekker, and others presented readers with a glimpse of a criminal underworld.[5] The message contained in rogue pamphlets was clear; read these works and do not fall foul of the artful designs of these sinister figures.

In Europe, there was the picaresque novel, named after the Spanish word *picaro* meaning 'rogue' or 'rascal'. The first of these novels was the anonymous *Lazarillo de Tormes* (1554). It is narrated in the first person and tells the story of Lázaro, a poor boy from Tejares near Salamanca, who spends his youth in the service of various masters. While Lázaro is not a criminal himself, throughout his life he comes into contact with many unsavoury characters. Having suffered what we might now term child abuse at the hands of several masters, who include a blind beggar man, a priest, and an impoverished gentleman, he enters the service of a church pardoner, which is someone who sells papal indulgences. The pardoner is a veritable crook who employs several tricks to con the pious out of their money. For example, one of his tricks is to heat a metal crucifix before saying Mass. When the village folk come to Mass and kiss the crucifix it burns them. The pardoner then tells them that if they have been burned by the cross they have been punished by God, and that the only way to mitigate this punishment is through buying an indulgence.[6]

More picaresque novels were published throughout the sixteenth and seventeenth centuries, and the genre eventually made an appearance in England. The first English rogue novel was Thomas Nashe's *The Unfortunate Traveller; or, The Life of Jack Wilton* (1594). Wilton is a page in the court of King Henry VIII in the year 1513, who tricks money out of the people he meets, but the story that he tells also shines a light on the shady, borderline criminal practices of the royal court. One of the most famous English rogue/picaresque novels appeared in the next century. Richard Head's *The English Rogue Described in the Life of Meriton Latroon* (1665) is a fictional, seriocomic depiction of roguery and excess in the life of the protagonist, Latroon, and his associates (the name Latroon is probably adapted from the Latin word 'latrones' meaning bandits and brigands). Latroon's depravity begins when he is a young boy. He beats the brains out of one of the turkeys that his father keeps.[7] Later on, he absconds from his parents' house and falls in with some gypsies who con people by reading their fortunes at markets and fairs.[8] Gypsies at this time were feared in Britain: they had arrived in the country relatively recently, and the first records of them appeared in Scotland in 1505, and in England in 1513. They were originally designated as 'Egyptians' because it was assumed that they had migrated from 'Little Egypt', which was an early modern term that referred to the Peloponnesian peninsula. They formed their own distinct subculture and very quickly acquired a reputation for idleness and criminality. What is more, because of their nomadic lifestyles, integration with local populations did not come easily. The government attempted to expel all gypsies from England with the passage of the Egyptians Act (1530) which declared that 'an outlandish people, calling themselves Egyptians, using no craft nor feat of merchandise … have monition to depart within sixteen days'.[9] This measure was unsuccessful and further legislation was passed against the gypsies in 1554, again to no avail. Although gypsies remained in Britain they were, for a long time, viewed with suspicion right down to the nineteenth century, when crime novelists often portrayed them as underworld figures.

Latroon progresses through life by becoming a thief, a beggar, an apprentice, a highwayman, and he fathers a number of illegitimate children. Prefaced to Head's story of vice and crime is a moral injunction:

> 'Read, but don't practice: for the author findes,
> They which live honest have most quiet mindes.
> *Dixero si quid forte jocosius hoc mihi juris*
> *Cum & enia dalis.*'[10]

There is no need to take this moral commandment too seriously, even though it is marketed as a book that would be useful for the reformation of licentious people.[11] Instead, the primary purpose of Head's *English Rogue* is to provide sensational, titillating, and violent entertainment.

As the fear of crime increased during the eighteenth century, we see popular culture giving expression to these anxieties. The novelist and magistrate of Westminster, Henry Fielding, for example, wrote a pamphlet entitled *An Enquiry into the Causes of the Great Increase of Robbers* (1751), in which, speaking of London, he says that,

> 'I make no doubt, but that the streets of this town, and the roads leading to it, will shortly be impassable without the utmost hazard; nor are we threatened with seeing less dangerous gangs of rogues among us, than those which the Italians call the banditti.'[12]

Many of these fears were connected to the increased urbanisation occurring in and around the metropolis. Furthermore, the rise of the middle classes, in tandem with the expansion of trade through Britain's growing empire, and later through gradual industrialisation, meant that people had more that was worth stealing. While London had always had unsavoury areas, the growth of poor quality housing with their courts and back alleys, as well as the fact that many people lived on the breadline, allowed crime to fester in these areas. This is why Fielding also remarked that,

> 'Whoever indeed considers the cities of London and Westminster, with the vast addition of suburbs; the great irregularity of their buildings, the immense number of lanes, alleys, courts, and bye-places, must think, that, had they been intended for the very purpose of concealment, they could

scarce have been better contrived. Upon such a view, the whole appears as a vast wood or forest, in which a thief may harbour with great security.'[13]

In addition, there was no police force during the eighteenth century. The capture and punishment of thieves was left to part time and unpaid constables, as well as some shady characters known as thief takers who 'controlled' crime in the capital by arranging for the return of stolen goods for a price. Even Fielding's Bow Street Runners, established in the 1740s, which was a small team of constables operating out of Bow Street Magistrate's Court, could not effectively combat what seemed to be an ever-rising crime wave, although it must be noted that some of the concern at the time was over-exaggerated. The government response to the seemingly increasing rate of crime was to increase number of capital statutes, and for this reason the eighteenth-century criminal code has been dubbed 'the bloody code'. In spite of the fact that 200 offences became capital felonies, however, most people were prosecuted under earlier laws enacted during the early modern period.

Concomitant with these concerns over rising crime rates was the lapse of the Licensing Act in 1695, in which the pre-publication censorship of printed works came to end. This resulted in a proliferation of literature of all kinds, with crime being one of the most popular genres. The sheer amount of crime writing published during the eighteenth century attests to the public interest in crime. Lincoln B. Faller, a scholar who has written extensively on the genre, records that the British Library alone contains over 2,000 criminal biographies.[14] And all classes enjoyed such entertainment. The works by Smith and Johnson, which are compendiums of short biographies of notorious criminals, were published in folio format with fine engravings. Shorter pamphlets were published which told the lives of individual criminals, and these could sell for anything between fourpence and a shilling. Broadsides containing the supposed 'Last Dying Speech' of an offender were sold at public executions, while periodicals such as *The Proceedings of the Old Bailey* provided readers with news of the latest notorious trials occurring in the capital.

Even novelists capitalised upon the public's interest in crime. Daniel Defoe, the author of the first English novel, *Robinson Crusoe* (1719), wrote several novels which drew inspiration from picaresque fiction and criminal biography such as *Colonel Jack* (1722), *Moll Flanders* (1722), and *Roxana: The Fortunate Mistress* (1724). If we take a brief look at the full title of *Moll Flanders*, we can see the influence of earlier picaresque and rogue literature:

> *'The Fortunes and Misfortunes of the Famous Moll Flanders Who was born in Newgate, and during a Life of Continu'd Variety for Threescore Years, besides her Childhood, was Twelve Years a Whore, five times a Wife (whereof once to her brother) Twelve Years a Thief, Eight Years a Transported Felon in Virginia, at last grew Rich, Liv'd Honest and died a Penitent.'*

Eighteenth-century works often had long titles like the one above, and they functioned as the blurb does on a modern book, giving a brief overview of what the reader can expect. Told in the first person, Defoe's *Moll Flanders* is the story of a marginalised woman progressing through life, becoming a criminal, until at last, in true picaresque style, she redeems herself by living honestly. Some late nineteenth and early twentieth century scholars in the past thought that Charles Johnson was one of Defoe's pseudonyms, and that it was he who wrote some of Johnson's works such as his *History of the Highwaymen* as well as *A General and True History of the Robberies and Murders of the Most Notorious Pyrates* (1724). However, concerns have been raised over this by modern literary critics, and two scholars in particular, P.N. Furbank and W.R. Owens, have attempted to de-attribute many works that have hitherto been assumed to have been written by Defoe. It does not help modern researchers that Defoe himself made no attempt to distance himself from works attributed to him, as he once said that,

> 'My name has been hackney'd about the street by the hawkers and about the coffeehouse by the politicians, at such a rate, as no patience could bear. One man will swear to the style; another to this or that expression; another to the way of printing; and all so positive, that it is to no purpose to oppose it.'[15]

Later in the century, Fielding wrote *Jonathan Wild* (1743), a novel based upon the life of the eponymous thief taker, while another eighteenth-century author, Tobias Smollett, also drew upon the picaresque in *The Adventures of Peregrine Pickle* (1751). Even the renowned novelist Walter Scott, an avid collector of criminal biographies (his copy of *The Highland Rogue* is currently on display at Abbotsford Museum visitors' centre), drew upon the genre for two of his novels; *Rob Roy* (1818) and *The Pirate* (1822).

Traces of criminal biography can be found to have influenced Scott's portrayal of Robin Hood in *Ivanhoe* (1819).[16]

Much of what we know about early modern highwaymen comes from these now forgotten seventeenth and eighteenth century sources. In this collection, we will meet a variety of criminals from the medieval period to the eighteenth century whose lives were retold in Georgian biographies. Without further ado, let us now meet Robin Hood, the most famous English robber.

Chapter 1

Robin Hood: 'That Celebrated English Outlaw'

'In this our spacious isle I think there is not one,
But he of ROBIN HOOD hath heard, and Little John;
And to the end of time the tales shall ne'er be done
Of Scarlock, George-a-Green, and Much the Miller's son,
Of Tuck, the merry friar, which many a sermon made
In praise of ROBIN HOOD, his out-laws, and their trade.'
Michael Drayton, *Poly-Olbion* (1612)

'Honour to the old bow-string!
Honour to the bugle-horn!
Honour to the woods unshorn!
Honour to the Lincoln green!
Honour to the archer keen!
Honour to tight little John,
And the horse he rode upon!
Honour to bold Robin Hood,
Sleeping in the underwood!
Honour to Maid Marian,
And to all the Sherwood-clan!'
John Keats, *Robin Hood:*
To a Friend (1818)

Everybody in Britain has heard of Robin Hood. He is the archetype of the noble robber who steals from the rich and gives to the poor. According to the legend, his true love is a woman named Marian. His fellow outlaws include Little John, Will Scarlet, Allen-a-Dale, and Friar Tuck. His arch enemies are the Sheriff of Nottingham, Guy of Gisborne, and Prince John. The story of Robin Hood has been immortalised in books, films, and

1

television series, and at the time of writing, there is a movie forthcoming starring Taron Egerton as the titular hero. Thus, it seems Drayton's prophecy that 'until the end of time the tales shall ne'er be done' will continue to ring true. This chapter briefly discusses some of the historical outlaws whom researchers have identified as being possible candidates for the 'real' Robin Hood.

We will never know if there was an outlaw named Robin Hood who inspired the stories that were subsequently told about him. There will never be a definitive answer simply due to the paucity of evidence surrounding his life. That said, this has not stopped people attempting to identify a historical outlaw. Likely candidates for a real Robin Hood have been identified. The late Professor James C. Holt in *Robin Hood* (1982), believed that a man listed in the Yorkshire Assize Rolls between 1225 and 1226 as 'Robert Hod, fugitive' is *probably* the man whose life gave rise to the legend. The same outlaw turns up years later under the nickname of 'Hobbehod'. There are several other candidates who have, at one time or another, been identified as the real Robin Hood. Among them is one Robert of Wetherby who is listed in the Court Rolls as 'outlaw and evildoer of our land'. Other potential candidates include a Robert Hood from Cirencester who, sometime between 1215 and 1216 murdered a man named Ralph in the local Abbott's garden. And in 1354 there was a Robin Hood who was incarcerated in Rockingham gaol for forest offences. A Robin Hood from Wakefield was identified in medieval records by a nineteenth century antiquary, Joseph Hunter (1783-1861). Hunter was appointed as the Assistant Keeper of the Public Record Office, or National Archives as we know it today. In a tract entitled *The Great Hero of the Ancient Minstrelsy of England, Robin Hood*, (1852), he argued that Robin Hood was from Wakefield. Hunter aimed to fit known facts to the early tales of Robin Hood. He first identified a Robert Hood who with his wife Matilda appears in the Court Rolls of the manor of Wakefield in 1316 and 1317. Without any evidence, he argued that this Robert Hood became an outlaw between this time and 1324, when Hunter discovered that there was a *valet de chambre* to Edward II named Robyn Hode. For Hunter, this seemed to confirm that that this man was the same Robin who enters into the King's service at the end of the fifteenth-century poem *A Gest of Robyn Hode*, when the King travels into the forest and meets Robin, and asks him to join his service. There are two problems with this approach; there is no indication that this Robyn Hode from 1324 was ever an outlaw; the idea of a monarch going into the woods, as the king does at the end of the *Gest*, was a common trope in medieval ballads, and it is highly unlikely that the

King ever went incognito among the populace. This has not stopped some local historians from sticking to Hunter's assertions that Robin Hood was a man from Wakefield. To say that the real Robin Hood was from Wakefield, however, is to mix shaky historical methodology with wishful thinking. The fact of the matter is this; yes, there was a man named Robin Hood who lived in Wakefield, but we do not know if he was an outlaw. Another thing which complicates the search for a historical thief is the fact that the name of Robin Hood was often used as an alias by criminals in the late medieval period, and it was used by a variety of people whose actions challenged state authority. In 1448, a mob in Norfolk chanted 'We are Robynhodesmen' as they threatened to kill a local official. In 1498, Roger Marshall appeared in court, having been charged with inciting over 100 people to riot. Surviving records indicate that Marshall used the alias of Robin Hood. Perhaps even the earliest mention of Robin Hood in court records, then, was simply an alias.

Thus, it is near impossible for anybody to identify a historical outlaw whose life and deeds match those of the legendary Robin Hood. Historians pursuing the matter really are dealing with scraps of information such as little notes in court rolls, complicated by the fact that criminals often used the name of Robin Hood as an alias. The very paucity of evidence regarding a real outlaw, however, has allowed the legend to grow over time, and be adapted continually by different people in different ages. Thankfully, academic scholarship has now moved beyond trying to identify a historical outlaw, and this is a move in the right direction. In the words of Professor Alexander Kaufman, 'the origins of Robin Hood the person and his original context are perhaps best left to those individuals who wish to search for that which is forever to be a quest'.[17] The impossibility of tracing a historical Robin Hood, however, does not prevent us from constructing a literary biography of his portrayals in literature from the medieval period to the present.

Stories about Robin Hood circulated at an early period of English history. In the B text of William Langland's poem *The Vision of Piers the Plowman* (c.1370), we meet a lazy clergyman named Sloth. Poor Sloth is not a very good cleric. He cannot read or write and he does not even know his Lord's Prayer by heart. However, the one thing that he can recite from memory is 'rymes of Robyn Hode':

> 'I can noughte parfitly my Paternoster as the prest it syngeth,
> But I can rymes of Robyn Hode, and Randalf Erle of Chestre.'

These words from are the first literary reference to Robin Hood. They make clear that during this period 'rymes of Robyn Hode', were in circulation. Transmission of these tales was often by word of mouth, for England was not a predominantly literate society in the fourteenth century as the skill of reading and writing was mainly confined to members of the Church and the upper classes. In time, these 'rymes of Robyn Hode' were written down. We have four surviving examples of these early rhymes, or ballads, of Robin Hood, and these are: *Robin Hood and the Monk* which survives in manuscript form and is dated c.1450; *Robin Hood and the Potter*, which survives in a single manuscript of popular and moral poems that can be dated to c.1500; *Robin Hood and Guy of Gisborne* is an early modern poem, but the story dates from the late-medieval period; and there is *A Gest of Robyn Hode*, which is dated c.1450 but only survives in printed copies from the sixteenth century.

The Robin Hood of these early ballads is very different from the outlaw that we would recognise today. While modern audiences are used to seeing Robin Hood portrayed as the dispossessed Earl of Huntingdon, Robin is not a nobleman in these early texts but is described as a 'yeoman'. Broadly speaking, a yeoman was a member of the medieval middle classes, for want of a better term, occupying a social position between the aristocracy and the peasantry:

> 'Lythe and listin, gentilmen,
> That be of frebore blode;
> I shall you tel of a gode yeman,
> His name was Robyn Hode.'
>
> [Attend and listen, gentlemen,
> That are of freeborn blood;
> I shall tell you of a good yeoman,
> His name was Robin Hood][18]

It is in the *Gest* that we first see hints of Robin having a social mission. The poem is divided into eight 'fyttes', and in the first, as we saw in the introduction, Robin sets out a code of conduct for the outlaws, telling them to not to harm women or ploughmen, but permitting them to steal from corrupt clergymen and sheriffs. The *Gest* is the most significant of all the medieval texts. It is also the longest Robin Hood poem, standing at nearly 2,000 lines, and appears to have been constructed from a variety of existing tales to which somebody, at some point, endeavoured to give unity. It is a type of the 'good outlaw' tale. Robin will help poor, honest people whom he meets; the first 'fytte' (section) of the poem sees him lending money to an impoverished knight named Sir Richard of the Lee, whose lands have been mortgaged to pay a debt to the Abbot of St. Mary's in York. Later on in this poem, many familiar scenes occur, such as the archery contest and his meeting with the King and subsequent pardon. At the end of the poem, Robin falls ill and goes to Kirklees Priory to be bled. The prioress, in league with Sir Roger of Doncaster, bleeds him to death. The poem then ends with a benediction:

> 'Cryst have mercy on his soule
> That dyed upon the rod.
> For was a good outlawe,
> And dyde pore men moch gode.'

> [Christ have mercy on his soule
> The died upon the cross.
> For he was a good outlaw,
> And did poor men much good].[19]

Although the idea that Robin steals from the rich and gives to the poor is not fully articulated in the poem (it was not until John Stowe's *Annales of England* in 1592 that this idea would become current), it is in the *Gest* that we first get the idea that Robin is kind to the poor and 'dyde pore men moch gode'.

In the other early ballads, all of Robin's fellow outlaws such as Little John and Much the Miller's son hail from the same social class of yeomanry. And Robin and his men are quite violent characters; in *Robin Hood and Guy of Gisborne*, he cuts off Guy's head, mutilates his face with a knife, and sticks his head upon the end of his bow:

> 'Robin thought on our Ladye deere,
> And soone leapt up againe,
> And thus he came with an awkwarde stroke,
> Good Sir Guy he has slayne.

> He tooke Sir Guy's head by the hayre,
> And stickt itt upon his bowes end:
> "Thou has beene a traytor all thy liffe,
> Which thing must have an ende."

Robin pulled forth an Irish kniffe,
And nicked Sir Guy in the face,
That hee was never on a woman borne,
Could tell who Sir Guye was.'[20]

Having said this, the violence is justified to a certain extent as Guy is a bounty hunter hired by the Sheriff in order to capture and kill Robin Hood. In *Robin Hood and the Monk*, two of Robin's men, Much the Miller's son and Little John, kill a travelling monk and his young page:

'John smote of the munkis hed,
No longer wolde he dwell;
So did Moch the litull page,
For ferd lest he wolde tell.'

[John cut off the monk's head,
No longer would he live,
Much did the same to the little page,
For fear that he would tell].[21]

There are also characters whom we would count as staples of the Robin Hood legend today that actually appear nowhere in these early texts. Maid Marian is conspicuous by her absence in all of the Medieval poems. In fact, Robin has no love interest at all. Marian entered the legend via a different route to the ballads. The first time that two people named Robin and Marian were associated together was in a French pastoral play entitled *Jeu de Robin et Marion*, dating from c.1282. It is unclear, however, whether the Robin and Marian of this play were understood to be outlaws. There is certainly no proven link between the play and the Robin Hood tradition. We do know, however, that Marian appears alongside the 'proper' Robin Hood in sixteenth-century Tudor May Day celebrations. It seems from thence she made her way into Anthony Munday's two plays *The Downfall of Robert, Earle of Huntington* and *The Death of Robert, Earle of Huntingdon* written between 1597 and 1598. Marian's place in the legend, however, is only really cemented in the nineteenth century, when a short novella by Thomas Love Peacock entitled *Maid Marian*, was published in 1822.

Robin moved up in the world during the seventeenth century. In the plays by Anthony Munday, Robin is cast for the first time as an earl. There was no precedent in the medieval ballad tradition for this. Munday did this because he was catering to a primarily aristocratic audience. Although largely forgotten about today outside of academic circles, these plays established a new narrative in the Robin Hood legend: Robin is depicted as an aristocrat; he is outlawed because of a plot against him by rival courtiers; and instead of having been a bold rebel, the reason that Robin is outlawed is because he has stayed loyal to King Richard. Hence any subversive political traits are extracted from his character. This was at a time when the established order was very shaky. Elizabeth I was old, London had experienced intermittent riots, and in the year that the plays were printed, 1601, the Earl of Essex mounted his rebellion. Thus, instead of challenging the establishment, in these plays Robin becomes an upholder of the established order.

During the seventeenth century, the Robin Hood legend was kept alive in cheaply printed and forgettable broadside ballads and chapbooks. Were it not for Joseph Ritson's *Robin Hood: A Collection of All the Ancient Poems, Songs, and Ballads* (1795), Robin's fame might have gone the way of other now largely forgotten medieval outlaws such as Adam Bell. Ritson (1752–1803) was born in Stockton-on-Tees and was a conveyancer by trade. In his spare time, however, he was an antiquary. He was interested, not in the 'high' culture of people in times past, but that of the common people. He published many collections of ancient ballads and songs such as *A Select Collection of English Songs* (1783) and *Pieces of Ancient Popular Poetry* (1791). And he quickly established himself as an authority on many historical subjects, owing to his willingness to seek out obscure primary sources from archives and libraries across the country. He was also cantankerous, and fiercely critical of his rivals such as Thomas Percy who took it upon himself to edit and 'refine' Old and Middle English texts. Ritson's work is significant in the overall development of the Robin Hood legend because, as his title suggests, he collected together and made accessible in printed form every Robin Hood text he could find ranging from the Middle Ages to the nineteenth century. The most important part of Ritson's work was the section entitled 'The Life of Robin Hood' which he prefixed to the collection of ballads. In this, Ritson laid down the 'facts' of the legend, saying:

'Robin Hood was born at Locksley, in the County of Nottingham, in the reign of King Henry the Second, and about the year of Christ 1160. His extraction was noble ... he is frequently styled, and commonly reputed to have been Earl of Huntingdon.'[22]

With respect to Robin's character, Ritson says that:

> 'It is sufficiently evident that he was active, brave, prudent; possessed of uncommon bodyly [sic] strength, and considerable military skill; just, generous, benevolent, faithful, and beloved or revered by his followers and adherents for his excellent and amiable qualities.'[23]

Another thing about Ritson is that he is a bit of an armchair revolutionary. His letters from the 1790s are full of praise for the French Revolution and Ritson reimagines Robin Hood as a medieval revolutionary, almost a Wat Tyler type of figure:

> 'In these forests, and with [his] company, he for many years reigned like an independent sovereign; at perpetual war, indeed, with the king of England, and all his subjects, with an exception, however, of the poor and needy, and such as were 'desolate and oppressed,' or stood in need of his protection.'[24]

And finally, Ritson tells us that Robin steals from the rich and gives to the poor:

> 'That our hero and his companions, while they lived in the woods, had recourse to robbery for their better support, is neither to be concealed nor to be denied [sic]. Testimonies to this purpose, indeed, would be equally endless and unnecessary [...] But it is to be remembered ... that, in these exertions, he took away the goods of rich men only; never killing any person, unless he was attacked or resisted: that he would never suffer a woman to be maltreated; nor ever took anything from the poor, but charitably fed them with the wealth he drew from the abbots.'[25]

As we can see, the story of Robin Hood, due in large part to Ritson, is beginning to look familiar to the story which we see depicted on film and television today. Ritson died shortly after the publication of *Robin Hood*, but we know from his letters that he corresponded occasionally with a young Scotsman named Walter Scott. It was Scott who carried Ritson's portrayal of Robin Hood even further in his novel *Ivanhoe* (1819), radically transforming the legend in the process. Scott is perhaps the most famous of all Scottish novelists. Born in Edinburgh in 1771, after completing his studies he was articled to the legal profession through a friend of his father's. Throughout his life, however, in his leisure time he devoted himself to antiquarian pursuits, avidly reading scholarly works such as Percy's *Reliques* and Ritson's *Robin Hood*. With *Ivanhoe*, Scott made a departure from Scottish history by writing a novel set in England during the medieval period, and it is with *Ivanhoe* that Scott is said to have initiated the Medieval Revival of the early nineteenth century.

The novel is set during the 1190s, and England is in a parlous state, divided between the Normans and the Anglo-Saxons:

> 'A circumstance which tended greatly to enhance the tyranny of the nobility, and the sufferings of the inferior classes, arose from the consequences of the Conquest by William Duke of Normandy. Four generations had not sufficed to blend the hostile blood of the Normans and Anglo-Saxons, or to unite, by common language and mutual interests, two hostile races, one of which still felt the elation of triumph, while the other groaned under all the consequences of defeat.'[26]

The divisions between the Anglo-Saxons and the Normans come to a head while Richard I is captured by Leopold of Austria, and his brother John rules as Regent. John taxes the people heavily to pay King Richard's ransom. In reality, John is hoarding the money for himself, hoping to raise an army to overthrow the few remaining barons who support Richard, while buying the others off. Unbeknownst to John and his Templar henchmen, Richard has also returned to England in disguise. Richard finds his land in chaos: outlaws roam in the forest; the Normans oppress the good Saxons; Ivanhoe's father, Cedric, plans on using his brother Athelstane, who is descended from Saxon royalty, as a rallying point through whom the oppressed Saxons can rise up and overthrow their Norman conquerors. Recognising the parlous state of the country, the outlaw known as Robin of Locksley teams up with both Ivanhoe and King Richard and so that Richard can regain control of his kingdom and thereby unite the nation. Added into this plot are vividly exciting scenes; jousting tournaments, archery tournaments, damsels in distress, and epic sieges and battles. It is a piece of pure medieval spectacle.

Scott completely invented the idea that the Anglo-Saxons and the Normans were at odds with each other in the 1190s, but it is a notion that persists in modern portrayals. He did this because he had a message for nineteenth century readers; society does not have to be divided the way that it was in the 1190s. Scott argues that if all classes of society work together, they can overcome their differences. Medieval feudalism, where each class owed loyalty to the other, could be adapted for the nineteenth century. England in 1819 was a divided society. The end of the French Revolutionary and Napoleonic Wars (1793–1815) brought in its wake a trade and financial depression along with mass unemployment. In addition, the working classes and the middle classes were agitating for political reform. Issues came to a head in 1819, while Scott was working on *Ivanhoe*, in Manchester. Peaceful protesters had gathered in St Peter's Fields to hear radical campaigner Henry Hunt (1773–1835) speak upon the issue of parliamentary reform. However, the local magistrate ordered the yeomanry to charge the protesters. Estimates as to the number of people who died on the day vary between eleven and fifteen. Between 400 and 700 people were injured. Scott himself was horrified by this event, and the general state of the nation. Hence the reason that he wrote *Ivanhoe* was to create a shared sense of history around which all people could rally. This is why we see all classes of people working together. Through Robin Hood, says Walter Simeone, Scott shows that 'from the beginning of national history, ordinary men had an important role to play in the shaping of the nation … his novel dramatizes the idea of history in which the lowest in the social order are as important as the highest'.[27] Robin Hood is the saviour of the nation in *Ivanhoe*; the upper classes need the working classes as much as the working classes rely on their 'betters'. Simeone goes so far as to argue that our modern idea of Robin Hood was invented by Scott and not Ritson. Robin of Locksley in *Ivanhoe* is a freedom fighter first, and an outlaw second. Simeone's argument is justified when we consider that almost every modern portrayal sees Robin as a political fighter first, and a thief second. In fact, as in *Ivanhoe*, in film and television portrayals we rarely see Robin Hood robbing anybody. Indeed, Robin is only an outlaw in Scott's novel because he and his fellow Anglo-Saxon outlaws have been deprived of their political rights by the Normans. Out of all the heroes in Scott's novel, it is only Robin Hood who people remember.

The early nineteenth century was a good time for Robin Hood literature. The year 1818 saw John Keats and John Hamilton Reynolds write two Robin Hood poems each. In 1819, two novels featuring the outlaw hero came out; the anonymous *Robin Hood: A Tale of the Olden Time* (1819) and *Ivanhoe*. Neither of those novels, however, featured Robin's love interest,

Maid Marian. Marian's 'big break' came in 1822 with the publication of Thomas Love Peacock's novella *Maid Marian*. Peacock was a friend of Romantic writers such as Lord Byron and Mary Shelley. Indeed, it has been theorised by some critics that Robin and Marian in this novel are based upon Byron and Shelley. Although the publication date of the novella is 1822, all first editions carry a note to the effect that the majority of the work was written in 1818. The novel was originally intended as a satire on continental conservatism and its enthusiasm for all things feudal and medieval. After the Napoleonic Wars, many of the pre-Napoleonic governments were restored to power on the continent in places such as France, Italy, and Spain. These governments' legitimacy rested on flimsy bases, and some governments, such as that of Spain, attempted to re-impose a new type of feudalism. While the press in some continental countries was hailing the return of established monarchies and the *ancien regime*, Peacock was more critical. Through his novella he shows that man's aristocratic overlords have always been the same; greedy, violent, cynical, and self-interested.

Peacock's novel begins with the nuptials of Robert, Earl of Huntingdon and his lady Matilda. The wedding is interrupted by the Sheriff's men who seek to arrest him for 'forest treason'. Robin fights of the Sheriff's men and then takes to the woods, despoiling the Sheriff and his men of all their goods whenever they can. After resisting the advances of Prince John, Matilda joins Robin in Sherwood Forest and assumes the name of Maid Marian. Together, Robin and Marian effectively rule as King and Queen in the forest:

> 'Administering natural justice according to Robin's ideas of rectifying the inequalities of the human condition: raising genial dews from the bags of the rich and idle, and returning them in fertilising showers on the poor and industrious; an operation which more enlightened statesmen have happily reversed.'[28]

As Peacock's title suggests, Robin is the secondary character in the novel, with Marian being the main protagonist. However, she is no delicate little lady as she takes an active role in defending Sherwood – Robin's forest kingdom – from the depredations of the Sheriff. She takes an active role in defending her home from Prince John's soldiers, and even fights Richard I in disguise. Marian is unsuited to the domestic sphere of life, and longs to be out in the world, as she says herself that 'thick walls, dreary galleries, and tapestried chambers, were indifferent to me while I could leave them at pleasure, but have ever been hateful to me since they held me by force'.[29] Peacock thus crafts an image of Marian as a woman who is active, strong, and brave. In doing so he was rejecting nineteenth century gender conventions, in which the woman of a relationship was supposed to confine herself to the domestic sphere, which is why Marian in Peacock's novel is regarded as a proto-feminist portrayal of the heroine. Peacock set the tone for future interpretations of Maid Marian as a brave heroine. In Joaquim Stocqueler's *Maid Marian, the Forest Queen; A Companion to Robin Hood* (1849), Marian is presented again as a fighting woman. The paradox is that Marian as a character has never been adapted by feminist writers. Nevertheless, the representation of Marian as an action woman is an interpretation that has lasted until the age of Hollywood; *Robin Hood: Prince of Thieves* (1991), the BBC *Robin Hood* series (2006), and the Russell Crowe *Robin Hood* (2010) all portray Marian in a similar manner to the way that she is portrayed by Peacock.

The man who really brings together the ideas of both Scott and Peacock is an author who is relatively unknown today; Pierce Egan the Younger (1814–80). Egan was a prolific author who wrote a number of medievalist novels, most of which were sold in weekly penny instalments. His quite radical work, entitled *Robin Hood and Little John* (1840), tells the story of the hero from birth to death. Robin is a Saxon freedom fighter, with obvious influences from Scott's novel, but he is also at the same time a chivalric, almost 'Victorian' gentleman. But he is a gentleman who knows how to defend himself; Egan did not flinch from making his novels violent. He illustrated many of the scenes in his novel himself and the pages are full of arrows in people's eyes, limbs are cut off with swords, and there is a high body count. It is the perfect novel for a young male readership, even if Egan himself intended his novel to be read by adults as well. Egan's novel was highly successful, perhaps even more so than Scott's; published in weekly numbers originally and then bound together in one volume, the collected edition went through six editions, and was translated into French by Alexandre Dumas as *Les Prince des Voleurs* (1863), which was then retranslated back into English as two novels entitled *Robin Hood the Outlaw* and *The Prince of Thieves* (1904).

After Egan, the quality of Robin Hood novels declines somewhat. And there are some terrible, highly moralistic novels. Some of them were written by churchmen, and they are all overtly patriotic, stressing the duties of loyalty and service to the crown. Whereas the Robin Hood of earlier novels had always represented something of a challenge to the establishment, in this any subversive traits Robin has are totally neutered. He is now a thoroughly Victorian 'drawing room hero' – a gentleman, a worthy subject, and in some novels it is unclear whether he is an outlaw or not. The one exception to these late nineteenth century novels is perhaps Howard Pyle's *The Merry Adventures of Robin Hood* (1883). Until Pyle, most Robin Hood novels had followed Scott in portraying him as an Anglo-Saxon freedom fighter. But Pyle returned to the earlier ballads, and from them constructed quite a lengthy narrative, telling the story of Robin's life from birth to death. This was one of the more successful novels.

At the turn of the twentieth century, however, it is clear that the medium for telling tales of Robin Hood was shifting from the book to the screen. And no twentieth century Robin Hood novel has ever really had the power to truly have a lasting impact upon the tradition as Scott, Peacock, and Egan did. Robin Hood movies were released in 1912 and 1913,[30] but the first major Robin Hood movie was released in 1922 and starred Douglas Fairbanks in the title role. The idea of Robin wearing tights was something which Victorian actresses adopted so that they could, with propriety, show their legs on stage, but in the 1922 movie the semi-acrobatic costume allowed Fairbanks to make darting leaps from castle edges, and Robin becomes a true swashbuckling hero.[31]

The next major Robin Hood movie was Errol Flynn's *The Adventures of Robin Hood* (1938). Flynn's portrayal of Robin Hood is very much influenced by Fairbanks' movie and Walter Scott's novel. Robin Hood is an Anglo-Saxon freedom fighter, but he is more of an American hero than an English hero in this movie. And the movie endorses Franklin D. Roosevelt's New Deal, which can be seen in the oath that Robin makes the outlaws swear to:

> 'You the freemen of this forest swear to despoil the rich only to give to the poor, to shelter the old and the helpless, to protect all women rich and poor, Norman or Saxon, and swear to fight for a free England, to protect her loyally until the return of our king and sovereign Richard the Lionheart, and swear to fight to the death against all oppression.'

It is this American, populist vision of Robin Hood that has persisted in cinematic portrayals. Hollywood has always far outstripped the British Film industry in terms of quantity of output, if not in terms of quality.

Robin Hood is perhaps the perfect hero to be 'Americanised'; he is the man who stands up for the common man against the strong and powerful, much like an American superhero. There is the idea that Robin is a Lord, but on the whole cinematic portrayals of the outlaw myth are relatively classless, just as American society is supposed to be. Perhaps the most memorable American portrayal of the outlaw legend, for many at least, is the Kevin Costner movie *Robin Hood: Prince of Thieves*. So Americanised was it that the filmmakers seemingly never even made the effort to have key members of the cast speak with an English accent.

The most recent movie, *Robin Hood* (2010), starring Russell Crowe, although criticised by some reviewers, was an attempt at least to ground the story of Robin Hood in historical context by portraying Robin as a man who contributed to the sealing of Magna Carta in 1215. It is essentially what, if it was a superhero movie, might be termed an 'origins' story. It is not a tale of merry men in Lincoln Green costumes outsmarting the Sheriff, nor is it a tale full of big Hollywood set pieces. Instead it is a thoughtful tale of a man who leads the people to secure political rights from the King. So it is better thought out than previous cinematic portrayals have been.

Thus, the legend of Robin Hood has been adapted by countless authors and filmmakers throughout the ages. There may or may not have been a man whose life and deeds gave rise to the legend that was to become Robin Hood. We shall never know, mainly due to the lack of evidence surrounding his life. From early poems and rhymes, the legend rolled on, and acquired new features; in the fifteenth century Robin Hood was a bold yeoman forester; in the sixteenth century he became a member of the aristocracy; in the eighteenth century he was portrayed as both a wicked criminal and simultaneously praised as 'the celebrated English outlaw'; in the nineteenth century in *Ivanhoe*, he became an Anglo-Saxon freedom fighter, before becoming more or less an American hero due to his representation on film and television. It is difficult to know what further turns the legend of the outlaw of Sherwood will take but it is likely that, in the spirit of Michael Drayton's words that, until the end of time the tales will ne'er be done.

Chapter 2

Adam Bell, Clim of the Clough, and William of Cloudeslie

With hats pinned up and bow in hand,
All day most fiercely there they stand;
Like ghosts of Adam Bell and Clymme;
Sol sits for fear they'll shoot at him.

Sir William Davenant,
The Long Vacation in London (1673)

In the previous chapter we briefly encountered William Langland's masterpiece *Piers Plowman*, in which Sloth the lazy priest says that he does not know his Lord's Prayer, but he does know ballads of Robin Hood and Randalf, the Earl of Chester. Ultimately, scholars can only speculate as to who the latter man might have been as very few sources concerning him survive, although his connection with Robin Hood in the same line in Langland's poem suggests that he may too have been an outlaw who enjoyed recognition in medieval popular culture. Scholars do know, however, that around the same time that the 'rymes of Robyn Hode' flourished during the fourteenth century, tales of the eponymous outlaw and his men were rivalled in their fame and popularity by stories of another three outlaw archers; Adam Bell, Clim of the Clough, and William of Cloudeslie.

The tale of these three outlaws was first printed in 1536, and then reprinted half a dozen times throughout the sixteenth century. However, we know that stories of these men flourished before this time due to the fact that a Wiltshire court roll from 1432 lists an 'Adam Belle', 'Clim O' Cluw', and a 'William Cloudesle' as aliases that were used by local men; it is unclear whether the aliases were being used by criminals or rather by law-abiding citizens as a joke. As with Robin Hood, it is difficult to ascertain whether the stories of Adam Bell and his band were inspired by the exploits of real people. It is doubtful that they are, and in any case, finding such evidence for a real Adam Bell would forever be a quest. Let us take a look at the ballad of Adam Bell, however. The setting is Inglewood Forest, Cumbria, at some point during the late medieval period, and the ballad opens with a celebration of the natural world:

> 'Mery it was in grene forest,
> Amonge the leues grene,
> Wher that men walke east and west,
> With bowes and arrowes kene,
> To ryse the dere out of theyr denne
> Such sightes has ofte bene sene.'[32]

> ['Merry it was in the green forest,
> Among the green leaves,
> Where men walk east and west,
> With bows and arrows keen,
> To coax the deer out of their den,
> Such sights have often been seen']

This opening is similar to those found in fifteenth-century Robin Hood ballads such as *Robin Hood and the Potter*:

> 'In schomer when the leves spryng,
> The bloschems on every bowe,
> So mery doyt the berdys syng
> Yn wodes merey now.'

> ['In summer, when the leaves spring,
> The blossoms on every bowe,
> Merry do the birds sing,
> In merry woods now']33

Clearly the forest, in outlaw ballads, is envisaged as a place where men are free, and it is an environment in which food is plentiful. The idealised rural world of the outlaws sets their way of life in clear opposition to urban life. This is why Stephen Knight, who has undertaken extensive research into the early ballads of Robin Hood, argues that they were likely originally envisaged by those who composed them for a town-based audience. They represented a freedom from city life that was not available to urban dwellers.

In fact, there is always trouble in store for the outlaws whenever they leave the safety of the greenwood and venture into the town. While William is an outlaw, he is also a family man, and his wife and three children live in Carlisle, along with an old woman who William's family, out of the goodness of their hearts had taken in. William expresses a desire to go to the town because he has not seen his wife for about six months. This course of action is evidently against Adam's better judgement, for he warns William of the dangers involved in venturing into the town. Adam does not order him not to go, however, which highlights the democratic nature of this outlaw band, in contrast to a poem such as *A Gest of Robyn Hode*, in which Robin Hood is the clear and undisputed leader. In order to allay Adam's anxieties, William tells him that if he does not return by the next day, then it is safe to assume that he is either captured or dead.

Having arrived at Carlisle, William shares a meal with his wife and children. The old woman who lodges at the house, however, decides to betray William by going to see the Sheriff and alerting him to the fact that the outlaw has returned to Carlisle. The Sheriff then gathers a number of the townsfolk who congregate outside William's house demanding his surrender. To coax him out, they set fire to the house. His wife and children manage to escape as he gives himself up to the Justice and the Sheriff, who gloatingly says:

> 'Now, Cloudesle, sayd the hye justice,
> Thou shalt be hanged in hast.
> One vow shal I make, sayde the sherife,
> A payre of newe galowes shall I for thee make.
> And the gates of Caerlel shall be shutte,
> There shall no man come in thereat.
> Then shall not helpe Clim of the Cloughe,
> Nor yet shall Adam Bell.'

> ['"Now Cloudesley," said the High Justice,
> "You shall be hanged at last."
> "One vow I make to you," said the Sheriff,
> I make a pair of new gallows for you.
> And the gates of Carlisle will be shut,
> And none shall leave or enter.
> Clim of the Clough can't help you,
> Neither can Adam Bell."][34]

A gallows is prepared that very evening and the walls of the town are ordered to be shut so that nobody can enter or leave, in order that nobody can go and tell William's comrades the predicament he is in.

Early the next morning, the justice goes out to see that the gallows have been erected and that preparations for William's execution are going according to plan. At the foot of the gallows, a young boy approaches the Justice and asks why the gallows have been erected, whereupon he is told that it is to hang the notorious outlaw, William. The young lad decides to sneak out of the town through a small gap in the walls to go and warn Adam and Clim about their friend's imminent execution. Upon learning that their friend is in danger, Adam and Clim resolve to rescue him from the gallows.

Adam and Clim assume the identity of messengers coming with a letter from the king, and arriving at the gates of Carlisle, they demand to be admitted. The porter at the gates grants them entry. Realising they will need the keys to make their escape, they kill the porter, or as the ballad so eloquently puts it, they 'wrange hys necke in two.'[35] Adam then steals his keys and both of the outlaws dispose of the porter's body. They arrive at the marketplace just in time; William is already in the cart at the foot of the gallows with the noose around his neck. Adam and Clim shoot the Sheriff and the Justice, at which the townsfolk begin to flee. The Mayor of the town next appears with a number of armed men at his side, but Adam and the outlaws heroically fight them off, shooting all of their arrows and continuing the battle with swords. The remaining men pursue the outlaws, and so they decide to make a quick getaway through the castle gates. But as they clear the gates, Adam turns round to his pursuers, throws the keys at them, and sarcastically says:

> 'Haue here your keys, sayd Adam Bell,
> Mine office I here forsake,
> Yf you do by my council,
> A new porter do ye make.'

> ['"Here are your keys," said Adam,
> "This office I forsake,
> If you'll take my advice,
> You'll appoint a new porter."'][36]

In other words, this is Adam saying, 'oh, by the way, you will need a new porter'. It is the equivalent of the classic snipe that a superhero in a movie or comic might crack to his enemies in the heat of a fight.

The outlaws then reach their greenwood haven where they sit down and partake of a feast, but as they sit under the tree they can hear the sobs of a woman and children. It is William's wife lamenting her husband's execution (it seems that William is more concerned with food and ale than ascertaining the fate of his wife and children). But Alice is immensely happy to see her husband, and the outlaws then kill more deer to feed the extra mouths. Adam and the rest of the band then resolve to send William's wife and two youngest children to a nunnery while they and William's eldest son go to London and procure a pardon from the king.

When the outlaws and William's son arrive in the capital, they make the usual curtseys and beg for the king's forgiveness. The news of the outlaws' exploits has reached the king, and he is not impressed:

> 'Be ye those theues, then sayd our kyng,
> That men haue told of me?
> Here to God I make a vowe,
> Ye shall be hanged all three;
> Ye shall be dead without mercy,
> As I am kynge of this land.'

> ['Are you those thieves?' our king said,
> 'That men have told me of?
> I make a vow to God,
> All three of you shall be hanged,
> You will be dead without mercy,
> As I am king of this land.'[37]

The king's officers then lay hands upon all three of them. The outlaws again beg for forgiveness, but the king is having none of it. Even the queen intercedes on the outlaws' behalf for mercy to be shown to them, and after some hesitation the king submits to his wife's demands. He therefore decides to show them mercy, and invites the outlaws to dine with him. As they sit down, a messenger comes running into the hall with a message for the king. It is from Carlisle, and the letter bears the news of the Justice and the Sheriff's deaths:

> 'My hart is wonderous sore,
> Had I knowne of thys before;
> For I have graunted them grace,
> And that for thynketh me,

19

> But had I knowne all thys before,
> They had been hanged all three.'
>
> ['My heart is sore,
> And had I known of this before
> I had granted them grace
> All three of them would have been hanged']³⁸

In addition, the letter also contains news of the outlaws having killed the king's deer, as well as having shot numerous sergeants and men at arms. The king demands an end to the feast, and commands his archers and the outlaws to accompany him to an archery contest, saying to himself that 'I will see these fellows shoot!' The reason why the king thinks an archery contest is an appropriate method of punishment for the outlaws is left unclear in the ballad, and the episode may have been inserted because people during the medieval expected an archery contest in these stories; an archery contest also appears in *A Gest of Robyn Hode*, and in *Robin Hood and Guy of Gisborne*. As expected, the outlaws show themselves to be true masters of the bow, and as in many Robin Hood stories, William splits an arrow that is lodged in the centre of the butt. Upon seeing this, the king exclaims, 'thou art the best archer'. William then wants to show off his archery skills to a further degree; he tells the king that his son has accompanied him to London, and that he would like his son to stand in front of the butt with an apple on his head, and that he will shoot the apple. The king agrees, but warns him that, if the boy is harmed in any way, 'By him that dyed on a tree … I shall hange you all three.' The spectators begin praying that everything goes according to plan, and that the boy will not be harmed. William draws his bow, and lets his arrow fly.

> 'Thus Cloudesle clefte the apple in two,
> That many a man myght see;
> Ouer God's forbode, sayde the kinge,
> That thou shote at me!'
>
> ['Thus Cloudesley cleft the apple in two,
> That many a man might see;
> "God forbid," said the king,
> That you should ever shoot at me."]³⁹

The king is impressed; William has proved himself to be the best archer in the land, and his son is unharmed. Readers familiar with the story of the Swiss folk hero, William Tell, who supposedly lived in the early fourteenth century, will recognise this scenario, for he is likewise ordered by a local official to shoot an arrow placed on top of his son's head. Furthermore, similar stories that can be dated even earlier than those of Adam Bell and William Tell exist in folk tales from other nations. Saxo Grammaticus in the twelfth century *Gesta Danorum* relates the story of Palnatoki who is ordered by Harold Bluetooth to shoot an arrow that is on top of his son's head as proof of his marksmanship. The Scandinavian *Þiðrekssaga* from the thirteenth century similarly relates the tale of Egil who is ordered to carry out a similar task. The presence of such an episode in *Adam Bell, Clim of the Clough, and William of Cloudeslie* serves to remind us that we cannot look at medieval outlaw ballads as being purely factual, even if some historians in the past have attempted to fit the events related in outlaw poems to historical events.

The king is so impressed with the outlaws' archery skills that he pardons all of them at once. He makes William his 'chyfe rydere' in the north of the country, and grants him a salary of eighteen pence per day. The king then confers upon William the status of gentleman, and the king further asks if Adam and Clim will become yeomen of the king's chamber (a servant who was permitted to enter the royal bedroom). This is a lesser reward for Adam and Clim, for yeomen were beneath gentlemen in terms of rank during the late medieval period. There is also a reward in store for William's wife; the king invites her and the children to court, where she will be in charge of the royal nursery. The other way of seeing this episode at the end of the ballad, of course, is as an attempt by the king to contain these outlaws and keep them close by him, essentially as hostages, so that they might not continue their unlawful depredations. Nevertheless, Adam, Clim, and William and his family spend the remaining years of their lives in happiness by the king's side.

While stories Adam Bell and his comrades may have rivalled those of Robin Hood for fame and popularity during the late medieval and early modern periods, Adam's, Clim's, and William's 'literary afterlives' never reached the same heights as that of the Sherwood foresters. There were minor references to Adam Bell and Clim of the Clough in some early modern poems, such as the one by William Davenant, an extract of which prefaces this chapter. There has been speculation by scholars in the past that the following lines from Shakespeare's *Much Ado About Nothing* (c. 1599-98) relate to Adam Bell:

'Hang me in a bottle like a cat, and shoot at me, and he that hits me, let him be clapp'd on the shoulder, and call'd Adam.'

The three outlaws receive their most epic post medieval literary treatment during the nineteenth century, however; Pierce Egan the Younger also turned his pen to the story of Adam Bell and his men in another novel entitled *Adam Bell, or, The Archers of Englewood* (1842), the first edition of which he also illustrated. The novel was serialised when the Chartist movement was in full swing, when working-class men, along with some of their allies in the middle classes, were campaigning for the reform of the parliamentary system. They had six demands incorporated into their 'People's Charter', from which the movement took its name: universal male suffrage; a secret ballot; annual parliamentary elections; equal size constituencies; the abolition of the property qualification for MPs; and salaries for MPs. Ultimately, the Chartist movement failed, in spite of three petitions presented to Parliament in 1839, 1842, and 1848; there are exaggerated newspaper reports from the time which allege that the last petition was so large that the doors had to be taken off the entrance of Parliament to get it in.

Pierce Egan was heavily sympathetic to the Chartist movement, and in his novels, he highlights the plight of the downtrodden medieval peasants, who in reality represent the nineteenth-century working classes, as evinced by several comparisons Egan makes between the Middle Ages and his own time period. A previous novel of his entitled *Wat Tyler; or, The Rebellion of 1381* (1841) presents the eponymous leader of the so-called Peasants' Revolt as a man who fights for a 'Charter of Rights', and at Smithfield presents Richard II with a list of six demands. In *Adam Bell* there is further sympathy for the plight of the nineteenth century working classes. Egan draws upon the idea of racial conflict between the Anglo-Saxons and the Normans, which had been invented by Walter Scott in *Ivanhoe*. Scott's racialism, however, is adapted by Egan to represent class conflict; since 1066, the good Saxons 'were for the most part stripped of their political rights, and driven forth to destitution and beggary'; they are 'the poorest class ... divided and subdivided, that they might not unite and rise up en masse to destroy their oppressive conquerors.'[40] Thus, the outlaws are depicted as freedom fighters, fighting against tyrannical nobles. Unlike the government in the nineteenth century who rejected all three Chartist petitions, however, the king in Adam Bell begins 'growing weary of the rapacity of the Normans,' and instead he begins a process of reconciliation by granting honours and rewards to the Saxons. At the end, Adam Bell and his band are pardoned by the king and return to their families.

After Pierce Egan, there are very few references to Adam Bell in popular culture, save for a few mentions in late Victorian Robin Hood penny dreadfuls. Adam Bell did make one final appearance, however, in the cult television series *Robin of Sherwood* (1984–86). In an episode entitled *Adam Bell*, Bryan Marshall portrays the eponymous hero as an ageing outlaw who sacrifices his own life to help Robin rescue a boy from the Sheriff of Nottingham. It is doubtful, however, that Adam Bell and his gang will ever recoup their former glory. The fame of Adam Bell, Clim of the Clough, and William Cloudeslie has been forever eclipsed by that of Robin Hood.

Chapter 3

Gamaliel Ratsey: The Repentant Highwayman

Drinke not the nectar of your neighbours sweate,
Steale not at all they God dooth so command:
Whose laws to keepe thy souvraigne doth intreate,
Thy health it is, Gods law to vnderstand:
Obeying God, God shall all harmes preuent,
Keeping Kings peace, thy King is well content.

Anon. *Ratsey's Repentance,*
Which he wrote with his own
hand in New-gate (1605)

With the tale of Gamaliel Ratsey, we move out of the Middle Ages and take our history into the early modern period. Ratsey flourished during the late sixteenth century, but because there are no surviving quarter sessions or assize records, historians know very little about his life. The principal source of information about Ratsey's career comes from an early criminal biography entitled *The Life and Death of Gamaliel Ratsey, a Famous Theefe of England* (1605). Many early modern criminal accounts must be treated with a degree of scepticism, for it was not unknown for authors to make things up on occasion.

According to his biography, Ratsey was born in Market Deeping in Lincolnshire. His father was an esteemed merchant and in his biography is styled a 'gentleman'.[41] That a merchant in this period could appropriate this title for himself, and be so called by other people, is significant; during the medieval period, to be a gentleman, by and large, meant that one had to be 'of the gentry'; that is to say, that the term was primarily applied to male members of the class one rung on the ladder below the nobility, and it included knights, squires, and landowners. These people did not work with their hands as yeoman and the poor did. They were 'gentle men'. There was

24

a further dimension to the idea of the gentleman, however, because if a man was of gentle birth, to be classed as a gentleman he had to conduct himself like a 'gentle man'. The historian Maurice Keen argues that we can see prototypes of the gentleman in depictions of the Knight and the Franklin in the General Prologue to Geoffrey Chaucer's *Canterbury Tales*. Yet by the early modern period, there was a high degree of social mobility due to the rise of capitalism and the breakdown of feudalism. Merchants such as Ratsey's father could become immensely rich, and of course they could, should they desire, purchase land and thus aspire to the status of a gentleman. Thus, the boundaries of the term became porous. However, as with many of the generalisations that historians are forced to make in their studies, there are numerous caveats to this; one of these being that, while in terms of wealth merchants may have been able to enter the ranks of the gentry, there was often snobbery towards them from older, more established families.

Richard and his virtuous wife had several children and provided them all with a good education. Young Gamaliel proved to be an excellent scholar in his early years, but by his adolescence he grew tired of academic pursuits and expressed a desire to enter the army. Accordingly, he joined the Earl of Essex's army to fight in the Irish campaign during the Nine Years' War (1594-1603). The English had had a foothold in Ireland since the Middle Ages, but their presence there was restricted to the region known as 'the Pale' on the eastern coast, while Anglo-Irish lords held control over the Earldoms of Ormond, Desmond, Kildare, Munster, and Ulster. Throughout the sixteenth century, however, the English had been making advances into other parts of Ireland to which, unsurprisingly, the Irish objected. In 1594, two Irish chieftains, Hugh O'Neill and Hugh Roe O'Donnell, and their allies waged war against the English. The war did not end in the chieftains' favour, and by the time that James VI of Scotland assumed the English throne in 1603, it was clear that the English advance could not be stopped.

In 1603, also, Ratsey returned to England, and with few means of supporting himself turned to robbery. On his journey home, he passed through Spalding in Lincolnshire and stopped at an inn. Having ordered some refreshment, he sat down and began flirting with one of the servant girls. The maid then asked her mistress if Ratsey might be permitted to dine in the parlour with the regular customers. From here, he could properly spy out any opportunities for aggrandising himself that might present themselves. He did not have to work very hard, however, for after a short while a local farmer entered the parlour and began making small talk with the staff. Ratsey overheard that the farmer was due to pay a debt of £40 to another local gentleman after he had been to market. The money was kept in a sealed bag, and he asked the servant girl to keep hold of it and return it to him upon his return. After the farmer had gone, the girl returned to flirting with Ratsey. As soon as the girl's back was turned, however, Ratsey quickly grabbed the bag and went on his way. When he returned home, he buried the bag in his mother's orchard.

That evening, the farmer returned to the inn and asked the servant girl for his bag. It was gone; the farmer was understandably distressed and the girl was distraught that the apparently nice man who was flirting with her could have done such a thing. The pair of them went to a local judge and asked for a warrant to be drawn up for Ratsey's arrest, which was duly granted. He was apprehended by the local constable and, despite denying the charge, was thrown in gaol until he could be examined by a judge. Prisons in this period were temporary lock ups which were designed to hold the accused until their trial and sentence. The prisoner also had to pay for their own food and board. When he was taken, Ratsey had no money about his person, and needed some in order to eat. So when his mother came to visit him in the lock up, he told her about the whole affair and asked if she could dip into his store for him. Ratsey's family, it must be remembered, was on the whole a respectable one, even if Ratsey proved to be the black sheep. The author of Ratsey's biography even goes out of his way specifically to say that Ratsey's mother was virtuous. Her conscience was very conflicted at being asked to carry this task out for her son, and when she got back home she sought advice from her daughter, who then notified the father. The justice soon heard of the matter and began making arrangements that Ratsey should be examined. Knowing that the punishment for stealing over £40 would be severe, he began to make preparations for his escape. How he managed it nobody knows, and all that his biography records is that he escaped 'out of a very narrow passage in his shirt'.[42]

After his escape, Ratsey obviously could not return home. He therefore went to the house of an old friend who gave him some clothes and a little bit of money to get by with. He then made his way to London where he might live a life of crime and find other like-minded fellows. Contemporary writers perceived London as a hot bed of vice and iniquity, so much so that the fear of crime in this period contributed to the emergence of a new style of crime writing; rogue literature. For example, shortly after Ratsey was executed, Thomas Dekker in *The Belman of London* (1608) attempted to shed light on this emerging 'underworld' of crime, delineating the different species of criminal that an unlucky traveller could meet with in London. Much of this was lifted from an earlier account written by John Awdley entitled *The Fraternity of Vagabonds* (1561). The rogues that flourished in Tudor England, furthermore, were ruthless cut-throats (or so they were thought to be), who, unlike the forest outlaws of old, operated according to no moral code but were a law unto themselves. For example, 'ruffler' in Awdley's work would, for instance, 'goeth with a weapon to seek service, saying he hath been a servitor in the wars, and beggeth for his relief. But his chiefest trade is to rob poor wayfaring men and market women.'[43] The 'frater' would similarly 'prey [...] commonly upon poor women as they go to the markets'.[44] Furthermore, the 'whipjack' would target small tradesmen.[45] Alternatively, their victims could be of higher social status, just as the cheats in Gilbert Walker's *Manifest Detection of Diceplay* go about 'by day spoiling *gentlemen* of their inheritance' (emphasis added). This is not to say these early examples of crime writing depicted a 'true' image of criminality in the metropolis, but rather they were the cultural expression of the fear of crime at this period.

When he got to London, Ratsey encountered would-be thieves just like himself. The first man he met was named Henry Shorthose, who had also been raised in Market Deeping just like Ratsey. The two of them then met another man named George Snell, a career criminal who 'was twice burnt in the hand in Newgate for his bad conditions.'[46] Branding was a common punishment for petty thieves during the early modern period; as well as inflicting instantaneous and painful punishment upon the body of the offender, in an era before police mug shots it was also a means by which the authorities might identify someone who had reoffended. Together, these men began to rob travellers upon the highway north of London. Among their victims were two scholars from Cambridge University, as well as two woollen merchants from whom they stole £40.

Ratsey was not totally ruthless, however, and as all good outlaws should, on occasion they stole from the rich and gave to the poor. One day, Ratsey stopped an old man and a woman on the road between Cambridge and Huntingdon. He bade them stand and deliver, but the old man pleaded with him, saying that between them he and his wife they had nothing but one shilling and sixpence. The pair was on their way to the fair to sell the rest of their possessions in order to buy a cow. At first, Ratsey was having none of it, and commanded the man to hand him his purse. The old man did as he commanded and Ratsey, finding that the elderly man was being truthful, was evidently moved to pity. Ratsey gave the old man and woman forty shillings from his own stock of money. 'Thus did Ratsey leave the old man both lighter at heart, and heavier in purse than he found him,' records his biography. It is not known how true this episode in his biography is; although tempting to believe that is indeed so, it is likely invented. Tales of outlaws demanding money from people and then finding out that they are indeed as poor as they claim, and subsequently helping the paupers out by giving them money, were common in earlier outlaw ballads such as *A Gest of Robyn Hode*.

Ratsey committed further robberies, but he was not, according to his biographer, a trigger-happy highwayman. Indeed, all good highwaymen should try at all times to refrain from using violence. This would be the ideal standard of conduct for highwaymen in successive ages, especially during the seventeenth and eighteenth centuries when they adopted the social codes of civility and politeness. It was much better to rob someone by charming them, or conning them, rather than going in guns blazing. And so one day (very few specific dates are given in early criminal accounts) Ratsey spied a preacher travelling alone on Newmarket Heath, Suffolk, and decided to have some sport with him. He rode up to the preacher and asked where he was travelling, and when the preacher said where he was going, Ratsey exclaimed that he was going there as well (the place to which the preacher was travelling is not mentioned in the accounts). The preacher said that he would be glad of his company, and the pair began conversing on a range of matters. Eventually, the preacher asked Ratsey about his life story, to which he replied that he was a gentleman who had fallen upon hard times, and had almost fallen into a criminal course of life, until he met the preacher and was able to confess to him all that was going on in his life. Ratsey also told him that he was sure that the preacher would remember the parts of the Bible where it spoke about being charitable to the poor. This seemed to move the preacher somewhat, and he opened his purse and gave Ratsey £3. Ratsey was sure that the man had more money about him, however, and so his feigned tale of woe continued, and Ratsey said, 'my minde giues mee (I cannot tell what the reason is) that you have more money about you. If you have, it ill befits a man of your profession to dissemble, for that is a fault you much reprehend in others.' The preacher then revealed that he had a further £10 on him, which Ratsey asked to see. Accordingly, Ratsey was handed the preacher's purse and saw this was true. He kept the £10 for himself and handed the £3 back to the preacher, telling him that God would surely remember this kind deed of his on the day of judgement.

Further robberies continued until at last he was apprehended. At this point, Britain did not have an organised system of law enforcement. The late Tudor and early Stuart state relied on a network of parish constables who mainly performed a 'reactive' role in policing; they did not set out to detect crime but merely responded to victims' complaints after the offence had been committed. As such, often criminals had to be caught 'red-handed', so to speak. The other way that the authorities could get their hands on notorious criminals such as Ratsey, however, was to encourage certain thieves to turn King's (or Queen's) Evidence against their former accomplices. This is what happened in Ratsey's case; he, Snell, and Shorthose learnt that a gentleman who lived about seven miles from Bedford had recently come into possession of £100. Consequently, Ratsey's gang decided to rob the gentleman's house. As they were biding their time nearby, the gentleman's brother came riding out with the money in a bag. Ratsey and the gang chased after him and knocked the man off his horse. The gentleman's brother was no wimp, however, for he drew his sword and commenced fighting with Ratsey, injuring him quite badly. Our thief was only saved when Snell came running up behind to assist his accomplice. Seeing that it would be no use to continue fighting against three people, for Shorthose had now joined them, the gentleman's brother gave up the money. Ratsey, Snell, and Shorthose then made a quick escape.

A few weeks later, the trio met up at an inn in Southwark, London, where they divided the booty between themselves. A few days later, Snell was apprehended in a tavern in Duck Lane for having stolen a horse. Horse stealing was a serious offence, comparable to car theft in modern times; people depended upon horses for transport, for work, and in Tudor and Stuart times the theft of a horse almost guaranteed that the offender would be hanged. When he was taken before a judge, Snell pleaded for mercy, and said that if the judge would show him leniency then he would give the authorities an even greater prize; the notorious offender, Gamaliel Ratsey. Accordingly, Snell directed the authorities to Ratsey's location, where the latter was taken and thrown into Newgate gaol. Shorthose was still at liberty, and having heard about the arrests of his former comrades, he intended to go to Newgate incognito to see them. However, he was pointed out to the gaol keepers and arrested as well. The three of them were then removed to Bedford for trial and sentencing. At Bedford, Ratsey did make one attempt to escape, having managed to get free of his irons, but he was quickly retaken. And poor Snell never obtained the reprieve he had hoped for as all three men were found guilty and sentenced to be hanged on 20 March 1605.

Chapter 4

Captain James Hind: The Royalist Highwayman

'Tis he, the sadler's son, the butcher's boy,
His father's grief, and once his mother's joy.
Who run from [his] master, and to London came,
To seek his fortune, and to get a name.
Where he not long had been, but quickly made,
Himself a member of the cutter's trade,
And grew therein so excellent, that he
Soon commenc'd master of that companie:
And to this honour is recorded further,
The poor he robb'd not, nor committed murther.

Anon. *The English Gusman* (1652)

It is often at times of political upheaval that banditry and highway robbery flourish. The instability generated by various contests between different would-be emperors in the Roman Empire saw the emergence of the bandit chiefs, Bulla Felix, and Maternus (see appendix). During the seventeenth century, England experienced its first major revolution, and it is during this time that James Hind, one of the most famous English robbers, appeared on the scene. There had of course been events which we could describe as 'revolutionary', such as the De Montfort Rebellion the 1260s and the Peasants' Revolt in 1381. However, it was under Cromwell that the English actually got rid of their king, not as the result of a dynastic dispute or a revolt of the barons, but as the result of a popular rebellion. King Charles I ascended the throne of England in 1625, and almost from the beginning of his reign made a series of blunders which gradually turned a large majority of the ruling parliamentary elite against him. One of his first miscalculations was to demand tonnage and poundage, which were duties on luxury imports, to finance a military campaign against Spanish colonies in the Americas. Parliament grudgingly granted this with many conditions. But the campaign was so ill-managed that the funds generated from this were insufficient to meet the needs of the army. Consequently, in 1627, Charles attempted to extract a forced loan from the people, and began to imprison those who refused to pay it. This did not go down well in a country which, ever since the passage of Magna Carta in 1215, had written into its laws the stipulation that the king could not impose taxes without the consent of parliament. In response to the controversy over the forced loan, as well as other disputes with leading parliamentarians, Charles dissolved parliament and began a period of personal rule in 1629. Charles made further gaffes such as the levying of Ship Money from the nation in 1635. Historically, this had been a tax which only those living in coastal towns were obliged to pay, and even then it was usually collected only in times of war. While technically the raising of the tax was permitted because it fell under the remit of the Royal prerogative, popular discontent was growing. Charles even had John Hampden gaoled for non-payment, and the response to which was an outbreak of civil disturbance protesting against the king's abuse of royal power. Finally, unable to bend parliament to his will using 'soft' power, Charles raised his standard and declared war against parliament in 1642. A bloody civil war ensued. It was the Parliamentary forces that would be victorious, and the king, on the orders of Oliver Cromwell and some members of the Rump Parliament, was placed under house arrest and put on trial for treason. It was a virtual show trial, and it resulted in Charles losing his head.

Although Charles was executed, he had a great deal of support amongst the common people. Indeed, the historian Tim Harris points out that Charles's government knew how to manage public opinion, or take into consideration the sentiments of the general public, in spite of the fact that at this point the majority of people were excluded from the political process. Charles was helped in this regard by a flurry of Royalist pamphlets which were published by various writers supporting his cause, although the Parliamentarians did also publish their own propaganda. It is the groundswell of support from people in lower stations of life which accounts for Charles's popularity among robbers such as Hind, who allegedly only ever stole from Parliamentarians and, if certain accounts are to be believed, once robbed 'that infamous usurper Oliver Cromwell'.[47]

James Hind was born in Chipping Norton and was, strangely for this period, an only child.[48] His father's occupation was a saddler. He was sent to a local boarding school to receive a basic education, but he was not a good student 'for his minde fancied other things'.[49] It was during his schooldays that he apparently became attracted to a life of crime, for whenever news was heard of a crime in the local area, 'he would importunately enquire the manner of it, and delighted more in such relations, than in anything that tended to his book.'[50] This last part is probably an invention of the imaginative mind of the biographer, who was in all likelihood striving to present Hind as a person who throughout his whole life had a propensity to wickedness. Nevertheless, the school got frustrated with him and he was expelled after only a year. He was then apprenticed to a butcher in Worcester to learn a practical trade. As we will see in some other highwaymen narratives, there is an odd connection between the meat trade and the 'profession' of highway robbery. The historian, Peter Linebaugh, in *The London Hanged* (1991) states that a disproportionate number of those hanged at Tyburn for highway robbery were found to have been associated with the butchers' trade at some point in their lives. As well as Hind, we find that the notorious Dick Turpin also began his adult career as a butcher. Jack Sheppard temporarily assumed the identity of a butcher while he was lying low from the authorities. It seems that a willingness to cut animal flesh was thought, at the time, to be indicative of a 'bloody and barbarous disposition'.[51] Contemporary commentators such as the poet and essayist, Alexander Pope (1688–1744), argued that butchers' shops were the epitome of barbarity:

> I know nothing more shocking or horrid than the prospect of [butchers'] kitchens covered with blood, and filled with the cries of creatures expiring in tortures. It gives one an image of a giant's den in a romance, bestrewed with the scattered heads and mangled limbs of his victims.[52]

Later in the century, Joseph Ritson, an eccentric vegetarian, made the case that butchers became desensitised to violence:

> The butcher knocks down the stately ox with no more compassion than the blacksmith hammers a horse-shoe, and plunges his knife into the throat of an innocent lamb, with as little reluctance as the tailor sticks his needle into the collar of a coat.[53]

This was related to a wider cultural perceptions that cruelty to animals inevitably led to the development of a criminal personality. At the beginning of *The English Rogue* (1665), for instance, in his youth the protagonist, Meriton, bashes out the brains of one of his father's turkeys:

> Thus happen'd, my father kept commonly many turkeys; one among the rest could not endure a fight with a red coat, which I usually wore. But that which most of all exasperated my budding passion, was, his assaulting my bread and butter, and instead thereof, sometimes my hands; which caused my bloomy revenge to use this stratagem: I enticed him with a piece of custard (which I temptingly shewed him), not without some suspition of danger which fear suggested, might attend my treachery, and so led me to the orchard gate, which was made to shut with a pulley; he reaching in his head after me, I immediately clapt fast the gate, and so surprized my mortal foe: Then did I use that little strength I had, to beat his brains out with my cat-stick; which being done, I deplum'd his tayl, sticking those feathers in my bonnet, as the insulting trophies of my first and latest conquest. Such then was my pride, as I nothing but gazed up at them; which so tryed the weakness of mine eyes and so strain'd the optick nerves, that they ran a tilt at one another, as if they contended to share with me in my victory.[54]

The association between animal cruelty and criminality would be made more forcefully in William Hogarth's series of illustrations entitled *The Four Stages of Cruelty* (1751). The first image in the series, *The First Stage of Cruelty*, depicts a group of children and bystanders enjoying the sight of a dog mauling a cat. Elsewhere in the illustration, two cats are hanged by their tales from a street sign, and two other adolescents are sticking an arrow into a dog's rectum, while a poor bird is being blinded by with a red hot poker in her eye by two other youths. In order to cement the relationship between animal cruelty and criminality, Hogarth depicts a street artist drawing the instigator of this horrid event, young Tom Nero, being hanged on the gallows. Throughout the succeeding illustrations, Nero progresses through life committing various cruel acts until finally, he murders somebody. He is executed for this act, and in the final instalment, *The Reward of Cruelty*, his body is laid upon the surgeon's table being dissected. Perhaps to avenge the cruel treatment of his fellow canines in the earlier image, a dog can be seen eating Nero's heart that has fallen to the ground.

One of Hind's biographers tells us that, throughout his whole tenure as an apprentice butcher, he harboured thoughts of becoming a highway robber, for he is said to have constantly told his fellow apprentices that the life of a highway robber was more attractive than that of a butcher's boy. After the space of only one year, Hind absconded from his apprenticeship. He dared not tell his father, who would likely have been enraged with him for doing so. Instead, he visited his mother when she was home alone and asked if he could borrow some money from her with which to travel to London. His ever-indulgent mother gave him forty shillings, a substantial sum in the seventeenth century; Hind had assured her that he had a job waiting for him in the capital which he had obtained through his contacts. When he eventually arrived in London, he went straight to a tavern but became so inebriated that he was taken to a Compter to sleep it off for the night. It was during his first night in the lock up that he made the acquaintance of Thomas Allen, a notorious thief, who, finding that the two got on quite well, resolved to take the young Hind under his wing and teach him to become a highwayman. Allen and Hind then repaired to one of the low taverns to meet the rest of Allen's crew. Sensing Hind's apprehension, Allen said to him,

> 'I would have you be as my companion and friend, and not as a servant, neither do I look for any such respect as you do give me; you shall eat and drink as I do, and if I have money, you shall have part, and want none, and if I want, you must help to get some as well as you can.'[55]

Hind was subsequently sworn in as a member of Allen's criminal fraternity, and then the gang set about planning a robbery. All of them went to Shooter's Hill where they saw a gentleman and his servant travelling towards them, whereupon Allen instructed Hind to try his hand at his first highway robbery:

> 'Hind rides to them (being already tutor'd to the purpose) and bids them stand, and deliver such money as they had, otherwise he would presently be their death; the gentleman not willing to die, presently gave him ten pounds, which was all the gentleman had.'[56]

Yet Hind was not totally without a shred of human decency, for upon seeing that the £10 was all that the gentleman possessed, he gave him back forty shillings in order to defray the hapless victim's travelling expenses. And for both the robbery and the kindness shown to the victim, he received praise from Allen because 'he rob'd him with a grace'.

For many highwaymen throughout history, it was much easier to simply con someone out of their money than charge forward on the heath with pistols at the ready. And it is through trickery that Hind robbed his next victim. One evening he was alone at an inn in the countryside near London. One of his fellow customers noticed what a fine horse Hind possessed, and he enquired whether he would be willing to sell it for £20 in gold, along with the gentleman's gelding *gratis*. Hind acquiesced and both men went to bed seemingly happy with their bargain. In the morning, the gentleman decided to ride out with Hind, and while they were riding, Hind asked the man if he could ride his old horse so as to show him how to handle the animal. The naïve gentleman readily assented, and once Hind was back on his old horse, he simply sped off with the £20 and left the old gelding with the gentleman.

Prominent Royalists took a liking to Hind because he, allegedly, only robbed supporters of Cromwell and Lord Fairfax, who, along with Cromwell, led the war against the Royalists. Thus, in 1648, Hind presented himself to Sir William Compton (1625-63), and asked to be admitted into the army to serve the Royalist cause. He was given a commission and placed in charge of a regiment of foot. However, the Royalists found themselves besieged at Colchester for eleven weeks by Fairfax, and the Royalists were forced into submission. Hind managed to escape dressed as a seaman. Hind is even said by some later biographers to have robbed Oliver Cromwell, although this story is most likely fictional, and the account appears only in Smith's *Highwaymen*, and Smith portrays Hind as the scourge of Parliamentarians. Smith includes another, quite comical, episode of him robbing Hugh Peter (1599-1660), one of Cromwell's inner circle and an advocate for executing the King:

> 'Another time Captain Hind meeting with Hugh Peter in Enfield Chase, he commanded that celebrated regicide to stand and deliver. Whereupon he began to cudgel this bold robber with some parcels of scripture, saying *The eighth commandment commands that you should not steal; besides, it is said by Solomon, rob not the poor, because he is poor*. Then Hind recollecting what he could remember of his reading the Bible in his own minority, he began to pay the Presbyterian parson with his own weapon, saying, *Friend, if you had obeyed*

*God's precepts as you ought, you should not have presumed
to have wrested His Holy Word to a wrong sense, when you
took this text, Bind their Kings with chains, and their nobles
with fetters of iron, to aggravate the misfortunes of your royal
master, whom your cursed republican party unjustly murdered
before his own palace.'*[57]

Whether this episode actually ever happened or not is highly suspect, and
Smith frequently invented facts. Smith's 'history' of the highwaymen even
includes an entry upon those noted robbers, Sir John Falstaff and Colonel
Jack, who are fictional inventions of William Shakespeare and Daniel Defoe
respectively. History books in the eighteenth century often blended facts and
fiction, and many works of fiction marketed themselves as histories, so Smith
was not being deliberately disingenuous as his style of writing was in keeping
with contemporary literary practices.

It would be unfair, however, to say that Hind's army service was mere
opportunism, because he appears to have genuinely believed in the Royalist
cause. We know this, not only from accounts of what he said at his trial,
but also from the fact that he was friendly with senior Royalist figures such
as the Earl of Derby, whose house he visited on the Isle of Man, and who
turned a blind eye to Hind's robberies during the revolution. Although it
should be noted that, in spite of Smith's attempts to portray him as a robber
who only ever stole from parliamentarians, contemporary accounts reveal
that he was not so discriminating. He is said to have robbed lawyers, excise
men, and innkeepers of all political persuasions.

It is interesting that when Hind was finally arrested, he was charged,
not with highway robbery, which was a capital crime in itself, but with
treason against the Commonwealth of England. On 9 November 1651,
the Cromwellian authorities, through means not quite clear, ascertained
that he was living under the alias of Mr Brown and lodging at a barber's
in St. Dunstan's, London. It is probable that somebody who had served
with him in the army had recognised him and snitched on him. Thus, the
servants of the Speaker of the House of Commons visited the apartment
above the barber's shop and found Hind fast asleep. They woke him up
and arrested him, and then took him to the Speaker's house in Chancery
Lane to be confined until he could be examined the next morning. And
it was no ordinary judge at the Old Bailey who he was hauled before one
of the Judges who sat on the Council of State. There he was quizzed over
the nature of his relationship to Charles Stuart, the dead king, and upon

his Royalist sympathies. Hind responded by saying 'that he never saw the king, since the fight at Worcester, neither did he know of his getting off the field, but he was now glad to hear he had made so happy an escape.'[58] This enraged the Judge, who ordered that he be confined in Newgate, where he was guarded by four musketeers.

Further examinations along the same lines followed the day after in Newgate. Hind was only ever a minor Royalist figure, and it must have made for a pretty pointless examination. After this, he was condemned to die as a traitor by one of the most brutal forms of punishment in existence at this time; hanging, drawing, and quartering. This is a description of the punishment as recorded in the trial of Thomas Wallcot and John Rouse approximately three decades after Hind's death:

> 'Then sentence was passed, as followeth, *viz.* That they should return to the place from whence they came, from thence be drawn to the common place of execution upon hurdles, and there to be hanged by the necks, then cut down alive, their privy-members cut off, and bowels taken out to be burned before their faces, their heads to be severed from their bodies, and their bodies divided into four parts, to be disposed of as the King should think fit.'[59]

There are many supposed last speeches attributed to Hind which were allegedly written while he was in gaol awaiting execution. In one of these, he declares that he forgives his betrayers and those who sentenced him to death, and that he was never ashamed of his Royalist beliefs, '[for] I would have all men true to their principles'.[60] In his final hours, it is said in some accounts that he was visited by his parents as well as one of his boyhood friends, before going on to suffer an agonising death:

> *Thus this great derider did deride:*
> *Who liv'd by robbery, yet for treason dy'd.*

Many accounts of Hind's life were published almost immediately after his death. His life and exploits were even celebrated in cheap broadside ballads. One of the most notable ballads from the period was *Captain Hind's Progress and Ramble,* which appears to be of late seventeenth or early eighteenth century origin. There are several surviving copies of this song in the archives of the Bodleian Library. The song was set to the tune of a contemporary Robin Hood ballad entitled *Robin Hood Newly Reviv'd*, and comically glorifies Hind's life and misdeeds:

> He was the most frolicksome blade,
> His merriment still did gain him good will,
> Tho' long he had follow'd his trade.
> At length being taken for treason God-wot,
> With a hey down, etc.

> Against the long Parliament state,
> Our Captain was try'd condemn'd, and dyd.
> And thus he submitted to fate.
> And many more frolicks the Captain has play'd,
> With a hey down, etc.[61]

Hind further appears in the criminal biographies of Smith and Johnson in the Georgian era. Seventeenth-century biographies of James Hind such as *No Jest Like a True Iest* (1652) were reprinted throughout the eighteenth century. As time wore on, however, it seems that his legacy began to be forgotten. Unlike other historical thieves, surprisingly, he only appeared briefly in a two-part penny blood story entitled *The Adventures of Captain James Hind*, which appeared in *Lives of the Most Notorious Highwaymen Footpads and Murderers* in 1836. Thus, although Hind briefly rivalled Robin Hood for fame and notoriety in his day, by the Victorian period his star had well and truly faded.

Chapter 5

Claude Du Vall: The Ladies' Highwayman

Then being brought to justice-hall,
Try'd and condemn'd before them all,
Where many noble lords did come,
And Ladies for to hear my doom,
Then sentence pass'd without delay,
The halter first, and Tybourn last,
In one day, in one day.
Anon. *Devol's Last Farewell* (c.1660)

And yet the brave Du-Vall, vvhose name
Can never be vvorn out by fame,
That liv'd and dy'd, to leave behind
A great example to mankind;
That fell a publick Sacrifice
From ruine to preserve those fevv,
Who though born false, may be made true;
And teach the vvorld to be more just and vvise;
Ought not like vulgar ashes rest
Unmention'd in his silent Chest;
Not for his ovvn but publick interest.
He like a pious man some years before
Th' arrival of his fatal hour,
Made every day he had to live,
To his last minute a preparative.
Taught the vvild Arabs on the road
To act in a more gentle mode;
Take prizes more obligingly, than those
Who never had been bred Filous:

39

And hovv to hang in a more graceful fashion
Than e're vvas knovvn before to the dull English Nation
Samuel Butler, *To the Memory of the*
Most Renowned Du-Vall (1671)

While Dick Turpin is today considered to be the epitome of the gentlemanly robber, during the seventeenth century, this honour belonged to Claude Du Vall (1643–70). He was the progenitor of the image of the 'gallant highwayman' that emerged during the eighteenth century. Let us take a look the life of Du Vall, who was once styled, 'the most noted highwayman that ever was executed in Great Britain'.[62]

Du Vall was born in Bishopsgate, London, but emigrated to Domfront in Normandy, France, with his family at a very early age. His father was a miller and his mother was a tailor. According to Charles Johnson they were honest and respectable, as so many highwaymen's parents allegedly were in eighteenth-century crime writing, which had the effect of making their children's crimes all the more heinous to readers. Little is known of Du Vall's early life; we are told by various sources that his father attempted to bring him up as a good Catholic, even if his father rarely attended church himself. At the age of thirteen, he decided to leave home and seek his fortune, as it were, by travelling to Rouen. While there, he became acquainted with several English gentlemen who took a liking to him and allowed him to run errands for them.

After the Restoration of the Stuart monarchy in England in 1660, the English noble for whom he worked invited Du Vall to return with him, to which the latter readily assented. When in London, we are told in contemporary sources that he soon became addicted to drinking, whoring, and gambling, and that his wages were soon consumed through these vices. Whether this is true or not is hard to say; almost every criminal who appears in the annals of seventeenth- and eighteenth-century criminal biographies is said to be fond of the good life at some point in their lives. Be that as it may, it is because his wages were not sufficient to meet the expenses of his extravagant lifestyle that he decided to become a highwayman.

The best highwaymen are said to have some style; they disdain to participate in common burglary and instead opt to steal only from passengers in stage coaches. At all times, however, his manner is polite and civil, especially if he meets with ladies. *The Newgate Calendar*, which was compiled from various sources in the century after he lived, tells us that he was often charming women with chat up lines as he robbed them such as,

'"Those eyes of yours, madam, have undone me."

"I am captivated with that pretty good-natured smile."

"Oh, that I could by any means in the world recommend myself to your ladyship's notice!" – These, and a million of such expressions, full of flames, darts, racks, tortures, death, eyes, bubbies, waist, cheeks, etc., were much more familiar to him than his prayers, and he had the same fortune in the field of love as Marlborough had in that of war — viz. never to lay siege but he took the place.'[63]

And Du Vall certainly lived up to this ideal in one episode that occurred early in his career. He received word that a gentleman and his lady would be travelling to London in their carriage and carrying £400 on them. With his gang, he surrounded their carriage and commanded the driver to stop. He approached the window on horseback and addressed the pair, asking them to hand over their money. The lady said not a single word but played a short refrain on her flageolet. Upon seeing this, Du Vall asked the gentleman if he might have the honour of dancing with his wife. The man assented, perhaps more out of fear than out of good will. Du Vall then alighted from his horse, opened the carriage door, and helped the lady to step out. The pair then proceeded to dance while one of Du Vall's men provided the music. Afterwards, Du Vall assisted the lady back into her carriage. Du Vall then addressed the gentleman again, and politely asked him to pay for the music that had been provided. The man handed Du Vall a purse containing £100, at which Du Vall said that he could tell he was a very liberal and generous person and that the £100 he had just handed over had satisfied his debt on the remaining £300. He then gave the pair a password, and said that if he should meet with any more of his men on their journey, to tell them the password and they should not be harmed. However, before we think of him as being too gallant, let us note that he did not always behave with politeness and civility towards women; one time he stopped a coach full of women and robbed all of them. One of the women had a baby asleep in her arms; its bottle had a silver overlay and Du Vall snatched it from the child. In spite of the mother's and her friends' pleading, Du Vall was not to be swayed. He would have the silver bottle. It was only when one of his companions told him it was unbecoming of a gentleman to rob a baby that Du Vall give it back to the mother.

One thing that Du Vall did enjoy doing was playing practical jokes. He was travelling alone one day towards London and decided to stop at Beaconsfield. Upon entering the Crown Inn, he could see that a wake was going on. He asked to be shown to another room to leave the revellers in peace, but he asked the innkeeper what was occurring in the next room. From written records, it does not appear as though any local magnate had died, and it was probably another type of wake, not practised in England anymore, that rural parishes held annually to bring the community together. While Du Vall was enjoying some refreshment, he noticed a farmer enter the inn carrying a purse of what Du Vall judged must be holding at least £100. He then struck up a conversation with the young ostler and enquired who the farmer was. It turned out that the farmer was local but was known as a stingy and heartless fellow. Du Vall's mind was made up; he would rob the farmer of his money. The plan that Du Vall concocted with the boy is so ridiculous and far-fetched that one wonders whether it is true or not. The ostler went outside and covered the landlord's hound in a cowhide. He then attached antlers to the dog's head. The ostler then got a pair of ladders and a rope and climbed on top of the roof. The boy then proceeded to lower the disguised hound down through the chimney chute. Back in the interior of the inn, the jollity ceased as all the revellers could hear a strange howling coming from the fireplace, and suddenly a horned beast appeared and was let loose in the inn. Everyone thought it was a devil that had appeared from the depths of hell. All the revellers were frightened out of their wits and made for the door, knocking over glasses and bumping into each other in their efforts to get out of the building, the farmer included. While many Protestant and Elizabethan writers held the belief in the appearance of demons and fairies to be nothing more than Catholic superstition, such beliefs lingered in the rural areas of England. When the commotion in the tavern had died down, the farmer checked if he still had his purse. He did not. Du Vall had taken it and ridden away. The farmer was enraged but the assembled villagers surmised that the appearance of the demon and the missing money was punishment from God for his being a mean, miserly, and uncharitable old fellow, and Du Vall was never pursued.

One time near Windsor, Du Vall happened to meet with a man named Mr. Roper, who was King Charles II's Master of the Buckhounds (perhaps Edward Watson, 2nd Baron Rockingham, who died in 1689 and held the position at this point). Du Vall commanded the man to stand and deliver all the money he had on his person. Rockingham readily assented and handed Du Vall a purse containing 50 guineas. Even though Rockingham posed no threat to Du Vall, he decided that for good measure he would tie

Rockingham to a tree. Du Vall then rode away and Rockingham was only found by a chance by another aristocrat who had wandered his way on his afternoon hunt.

The following adventure may be true although it does not appear in one of the earliest accounts of Du Vall's life published in 1670 but only in later histories of the highwaymen by Alexander Smith. Nevertheless, it is interesting as an example of the playful tricks that were attributed to Du Vall. Highway robbery was becoming a nuisance for the British authorities, and Du Vall was singled out in several proclamations as being one of the most notorious. He therefore decided to retire to France and lie low for a while, hoping that things would blow over back home. In Paris, he lived it up and spent most of his days drinking and sleeping with prostitutes, or so he boasted at any rate. Soon he exhausted his supply of money and began concocting schemes to raise more funds. For whatever reason, he decided not to go robbing on the highway but to become a con-man instead. He approached a Jesuit priest, who was the confessor to the king of France, and told him that he was a poor scholar who had studied in Rome and Venice and had discovered the secret of alchemy; that is, he had found a method through which he could transform base metals into pure gold. Early chemists, or alchemists, truly believed that, if one could find the secret alchemical substance known as the philosopher's stone then one could transform any substance into gold. This was not a fringe belief held by a few crackpots; even respected scientists such as Isaac Newton were engaged in discovering the formula to create the stone.

Intrigued, the priest informed Du Vall that he would allow him to stay in his house, pay him a salary and provide him with anything he might require in order for him to carry out his 'scientific' experiments. Du Vall even promised him proof that he could do it. Unseen to the priest, he placed a small amount of gold inside some lead, and added a tiny bit of gunpowder into the molten liquid for effect. He then proceeded to melt all of it down, and during the process, due to the gunpowder, sparks flew which made the experiment look all the more impressive. When the fire had consumed most of the lead, all that remained was the gold. The priest was ecstatic and furnished Du Vall with even more money. This continued for a few weeks, and Du Vall gave several similar demonstrations to the priest. During this time the priest continually pressed him to write down his secret so, sensing that he could not keep this pretence up for long, one night he crept into the priest's bedroom and bound his hands and feet. He then ransacked the place of all gold and silver and made his way back to England.

For a highwayman who was so notorious that he became a legend in his own lifetime, one might expect the story of his capture and imprisonment to be one in which he heroically but forlornly fought off the authorities after a pistol fight, but the truth is rather more mundane. He had always been fond of a drink, and one of his favourite places was the Hole in the Wall, a public house in Chandos Street. In December 1669, he decided to take some refreshment there but because he had had a few too many drinks, he fell asleep in the tavern. He was apprehended there by a constable who immediately conveyed him to Newgate. A highwayman as infamous as he was appearing before the court meant that the inevitable outcome of his trial was death. While awaiting his execution, he entertained many visitors in gaol, and ladies, some of whom were high-ranking, came to pay their respects. In a copy of a letter found in his cell after his death, Du Vall paid homage to the various ladies of the court and the middling sorts who had comforted him in his final hours:

> 'I should be very ungrateful (which amongst persons of honour, is a greater crime than that for which I die) should I not acknowledge my obligation to you, fair English ladies. I could not have hoped that a person of my nation, birth, education, and Condition, could have had so many and powerful Charms, to captivate you all, and to tie you so firmly to my interest; that you have not abandon'd me in distress or in prison, that you have accompanied me to this place of Death, of Ignominious Death. From the Experience of your true Loves I speak it; nay I know I speak your Hearts, you could be content to die with me now, and even here, could you be assured of enjoying your beloved Du Vall in the other world. How mightily and how generously have you rewarded my little Services? Shall I ever forget that universal Consternation amongst you when I was taken, your frequent, your chargeable Visits to me at Newgate, your shreeks, your swoonings when I was Condemned, your zealous Intercession and Importunity for my Pardon? You could not have erected fairer Pillars of Honour and respect to me, had I been a Hercules, and could have got fifty Sons in a Night. It has been the Misfortune of several English Gentlemen, in the times of the late Usurpation, to die at this place upon the honourablest Occasion that ever presented its self, the indeavouring to restore their exil'd sovereign:

gentlemen indeed, who had ventured their Lives, and lost their Estates in the service of their prince; but they all died unlamented and uninterceded for, because they were English. How much greater therefore is my Obligation, whom you love better than your own Country-men, better than your own dear Husbands? Nevertheless, Ladies it does not grieve me, that your Intercession for my life prov'd ineffectual; for now I shall die with little pain, a healthful body, and I hope a prepared mind. For my Confessor has shewed me the Evil of my way, and wrought in me a true Repentance; witness these tears, these unfeigned tears. Had you prevail'd for my life, I must in gratitude have devoted it wholly to you, which yet would have been but short; for, had you been sound, I should have soon died of a consumption; if otherwise, of the pox.'[64]

Other contemporary sources say that this is not a copy of letter found in his cell but the words of the final speech he gave to the assembled multitudes on the scaffold at Tyburn.[65] Yet the sympathies of aristocratic ladies, and even that of Charles II, could not save Du Vall from the gallows. Thus, on 21 January 1670, at the age of 27, Claude Du Vall was hanged. His body was taken to Covent Garden churchyard to be buried and the following is a copy of the inscription that is carved on to his headstone:

Here lies Du Vall, Reader, if male thou art,
Look to thy purse. If female, to thy heart.
Much havoc has he made of both; for all
Men he made to stand, and women he made to fall
The second Conqueror of the Norman race,
Knights to his arm did yield, and ladies to his face.
Old Tyburn's glory; England's illustrious Thief,
Du Vall, the ladies' joy; Du Vall, the ladies' grief.[66]

Chapter 6

Sawney Beane: 'A Picture of Human Barbarity'

*In all ages, past and present, 'tis impossible for history to
parallize, or the age to come, for such unheard of cruelties,
and robberies, that were committed by one Sawney Beane,
a Scotchman, in the reign of King James the First, before he
came to the Crown of England.*
Alexander Smith, *The History and
Lives of Modern Rogues* (1726)

Lincoln B. Faller, an expert in eighteenth-century criminal biography, argues that literary representations of offenders during the early modern period generally fall into three categories; hero, buffoon, and brute.[67] We have encountered some of these types in this history already; as heroes we have legendary thieves such as Robin Hood, as well as little rascals like Jack Sheppard. Faller's concept can be applied to thieves today; as heroes we have men such as the Great Train Robber, Ronnie Biggs; as buffoons we have those that appear on television shows such as America's Dumbest Criminals, while for brutes we have John Wayne Gacy, Charles Manson, Moira Hindley and Ian Brady. For an example of a 'historical' brutish criminal, we turn now to the legend of Sawney Beane, a cannibal who supposedly lived in Scotland during the seventeenth century.

Beane was born in East Lothian, Scotland, at some point during the reign of King James VI of Scotland and I of England. His father was a hedger and ditcher, and brought young Sawney up to the same occupation. Charles Johnson tells us that, from a young age, Sawney was 'naturally vicious and idle'.[68] Disdaining any form of industrious employment, he and a local girl left his home town and settled in Galloway. Having no money, they made their dwelling in a cave on the seafront, the exact place of which is not determined. It was a large cave with 'many intricate windings and turnings which led to the extremity of the subterraneous dwelling, which would eventually become "the habitation of horrid cruelty".'[69]

Being an unskilled labourer, he had no trade to fall back on, and so Sawney and his wife took to robbing lonely travellers. In order to ensure that they would never be detected, the pair murdered everyone whom they robbed. At some point early on in their criminal careers, the pair decided that, rather than waste money on buying food, and risking detection and arrest for the handling of stolen goods, it would be much easier if they were to turn to the bodies of their victims for sustenance. They would cut up the bodies of their victims into little pieces which were then salted or pickled. The parts that they did not eat were unceremoniously cast out into the sea. Some versions of the tale say that they were so depraved that they did not spare men, women, or children.

Eventually, Sawney and his wife had a family, and they raised eight sons and six daughters. All of their children were taught from an early age to rob and kill travellers. As the whole family had little contact with the outside world, beyond the maiming and killing of strangers, the parents encouraged their sons and daughters to have sex with one another. Incest was rightly frowned upon by many during the eighteenth century, which is when biographies of Beane and his family begin to appear. Incest could, however, be common in some remote areas, even into the twentieth century. Laurie Lee in *Cider wiith Rosie* (1959) tells of how in the Slad Valley in the early decades of the twentieth century incest occurred among some families. Eventually, Sawney's whole diseased and deformed family amounted to forty-eight souls. Their robberies and murders were carried out in the following manner; a party of them would lie in wait in the hills and ambush the travellers, and if one of the victims escaped, they ran into another party of the Beane family waiting for them. By these means they ensured that nobody ever escaped. Indeed, they became ever bolder and more daring in their actions. When it was just Beane and his wife, they only ever attacked lone travellers, but with their increased numbers they were soon attacking parties of five or six armed men.

Nobody in the surrounding countryside could figure out why people were going missing. Many local innkeepers came under suspicion, for often the victims were last seen in their establishments. In order to avoid unfounded accusations, many of the innkeepers in the area shut up shop and moved elsewhere. This, of course, helped Beane and his depraved family even more, for travellers had to travel longer on their own and there were fewer safe havens for them.

However, Beane's reign of terror would eventually come to an end. While Scotland in the early modern period had little in the way of effective policing, contemporaries did place their faith in divine providence. It was, after all, a more religious age, and around the time that Sawney Beane is said to have lived, Thomas Beard and Thomas Taylor wrote *The Theatre of God's Judgements* (1597). Their work illuminates the ways in which a notorious offender would be caught and eventually be forced to face God's justice, even if the justice of men was ineffective:

> 'We see how hard it is for a murderer to escape without his reward: when the justice of man is either too blinde, that it cannot search out the truth, or too blunt, that it doth not strike with severity the man appointed unto death, then the justice of God riseth up.'[70]

Although Beard was a rather eccentric, Puritan fanatic, the idea that Divine Providence would eventually bring to light a murderer's crimes, even if it took years, is found in the writings of Sir John Fielding (1721–80). In *True Examples of the Interposition of Divine Providence in the Discovery and Punishment of Murder* (c. 1760), he argues that through Divine Providence, 'sooner or later all shall come to light'.[71] Beane had provoked God's wrath with his unnatural crimes, and he could not be allowed to continue in his wicked ways. One day, a man and his wife were travelling through some of the lonelier roads in Galloway on horseback. They looked like easy prey for the family, and in their usual manner the clan waited silently on the hills watching them pass by at a slow pace. Suddenly, some members of the family pounced upon the pair of travellers and pulled the wife off the horse onto the ground where she was instantly disembowelled. Meantime, although he was surrounded by the family of murderers, the husband was putting up a good fight and had not been dragged off his horse. Amazingly, he managed to get free of their clutches and quickly rode off. Some of the other family members were waiting for him further down the road, in accordance with their usual manner of robbing people in two parties, but the man courageously rode towards them and trampled one of the brutes underfoot as he fled.

Eventually the husband came across a party of men who were travelling home from the local fair. He related to them all that had happened and they accompanied him to where the attack took place. The villains had fled but his wife's badly mangled body was still laid on the ground, disembowelled.

Above: Engraving from *Robin Hood's Garland* (1685).

Below: John Bewick's illustration to *Robin Hood and Guy of Gisborne*, published in Joseph Ritson's *Robin Hood* (1795).

Above: John Bewick's illustration to *A Gest of Robyn Hode*, published in Joseph Ritson's *Robin Hood* (1795).

Below: John Bewick's illustration to *Robin Hood's Birth, Breeding, and Valour*, published in Joseph Ritson's *Robin Hood* (1795).

John Bewick's illustration to *Robin Hood and the Stranger*, published in Joseph Ritson's *Robin Hood* (1795).

John Bewick's illustration to *Robin Hood Rescuing Will Stutely*, published in Joseph Ritson's *Robin Hood* (1795).

Left: Pierce Egan's illustration of Adam Bell, Clym of the Clough, and William of Cloudeslie at the siege of Carlisle, published in Egan's eponymous penny blood in 1842.

Below left: Frontispiece to Richard Head's *The English Rogue* (1665).

Below right: Claude Du Vall (1643–70)

Right: A public whipping in the Sessions House Yard at the Old Bailey.

Below: The interior of the Old Bailey.

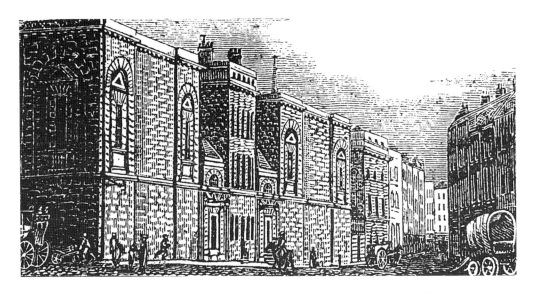

Above: Illustration of Newgate Gaol.

Left: Crowds gather to view a hanging outside of Newgate.

Right: Sir Walter Scott (1771–1832), the author of *Rob Roy* (1818) and *Ivanhoe* (1819).

Below left: Rob Roy (1671-1734).

Below right: Claude Du Vall dances with a lady whose carriage he stopped.

Above: Captain Macheath, the hero of John Gay's *The Beggar's Opera* and also of late-Victorian penny dreadfuls.

Left: Daniel Defoe (1660–1731)

Right: Henry Fielding (1707–54), the novelist and magistrate who established the Bow Street Runners.

Below left: Illustration of Bow Street Runners on the trail of a criminal.

Below right: Illustration of a highwaymen from Charles Macfarlane's *History of the Banditti* (1833)

Jack Sheppard carves his name into wood.

Jack Sheppard stealing in a church.

Jack Sheppard in a 'low' tavern.

Jack Sheppard and Edgworth Bess escape from Clerkenwell Prison.

Jack Sheppard faces off against Jonathan Wild.

Jonathan Wild and Robin of Bagshot.

Above: Sir James Thornhill painting Jack Sheppard.

Right: William Harrison Ainsworth (1805–82), author of *Rookwood* (1834) and *Jack Sheppard* (1839).

Left: Dick Turpin's Ride to York (I).

Below left: Dick Turpin's Ride to York (II).

Below right: Black Bess dies in sight of York Minster.

Right: A Jack Sheppard penny dreadful from the late-Victorian era.

Below: William Dodd composing *Thoughts in Prison* (1777) while imprisoned in Newgate.

Above left: The execution of William Dodd.

Above Right: Eugene Sue's highly influential novel about the Parisian underworld: *The Mysteries of Paris* (1842–43).

Left: The characters and crooks of London from G.W.M. Reynolds's *The Mysteries of London* (1844–46).

The entire party of men went straight to the sheriff at Glasgow and reported everything that had happened. The sheriff then related the events to James VI, who raised an army of 400 men to venture into the countryside and hunt down the depraved individuals.

After a long day searching, it seemed as though it might prove to be fruitless. However, the soldiers had several bloodhounds with them, and as the soldiers were walking on the seafront, the dogs began to bark when they passed outside the entrance to Sawney's cave. A large party entered the cave and what they saw shocked them:

> 'Legs, arms, thighs, hands, and feet, of men, women, and children, were suspended in rows like dried beef. Some limbs and other members were soaked in pickle; while a great mass of money, both of gold and silver, watches, rings, pistols, clothes, both woollen and linen, with an innumerable quantity of other articles, were either thrown together in heaps, or suspended upon the sides of the cave.'[72]

Sawney and his family were seized at once and marched to Edinburgh. They were locked up for the evening in the tollbooth. Given that their crimes were of the most heinous nature, and in the eyes of contemporaries, offensive to both man and God, James decided that they did not even deserve a trial. The whole family were executed in the morning; Beane and the other male members of the family had their penises, hands, and feet cut off, and were left to bleed to death, and the women were burnt alive.

The veracity of the tale is unclear, but a nineteenth century historian pointed out that Hector Boece, in *Historia Gentis Scotorum* (1527), records a similar tale of a Scottish brigand and his wife and children, who were condemned to death after it was proved that they killed and ate their prisoners. However, there are no records of innkeepers being wrongfully accused of murders in the Galloway region during the reign of James VI. The scholar and antiquary, Robert Pitcairn (1793-1855), could find no record of Beane or his alleged murders when he was compiling his multivolume *Ancient Criminal Trials in Scotland* (1833). In fact, although the tale was regularly reprinted in many of the *Lives of the Highwaymen* books and penny dreadfuls published throughout the nineteenth century, historians then did not think it worth the effort to even bother researching what was, to them at least, a so obviously contrived folk tale. That was until a novel by S.R. Crockett entitled *The Grey Man* (1896) claimed to have located Beane's cave of horrors. This led to renewed scholarly interest in the tale, although not all historians were impressed. An author known simply as Alba, in *Scottish Notes and Queries*, a now-defunct academic journal, argued in 1906 that the whole story of Sawney Beane was a fiction without any foundation whatever in fact. The author's choice of name is telling; he is a nationalist, and he further argued that the whole tale is one that was concocted by the English and 'Anglified Scots' to vilify his once proud nation.[73] In the next issue of the journal, another historian took issue with some of Alba's conclusions:

> 'The story of Sawney Beane – one of the most repulsive, incredible, and impossible stories that was ever penned – is not to be lightly dismissed as a fabrication ... "There's no smoke without fire" – as the proverb hath it. The gruesome tale undoubtedly rests on a basis of facts, which in course of time became overlaid (as such tales are apt to be) with a mass of fictitious details and horrific embellishments.'[74]

The original tale, the same author concludes, is likely to be the one recorded by Boece in the sixteenth century.

As the second author intimates, tales such as Sawney Beane's often have a kernel of truth about them. It is later authors who change them, adding new characters and settings, often to the point that the tale is no longer recognisable to that which has gone before. In the twentieth century, it was the horror movie maestro, Wes Craven who adapted Beane's story for Hollywood in *The Hills Have Eyes* (1977). In this film, a murderous, cannibalistic family ambushes a family travelling through the Nevada desert. Although the film did not do well at the box office, it has since become a cult classic. A sequel was produced in 1985, and a remake was released in 2006, to which another sequel was made in 2007. Although the story of Beane was Craven's primary inspiration for the movie, there are close parallels between Beane's story and the family of the Benders. Members of this family were married to one another and they terrorised travellers in Kansas between 1869 and 1872.

Surprisingly, there are very few academic studies about cannibalism, or to give it its scientific term, anthropophagy. Most people rightly regard it as a depraved crime, the epitome of savagery. There are several reports of Crusaders in the Holy Land turning to cannibalism in times of dearth. A text entitled *Richard Coeur de Lion* (c.1300) says that during the Third

Crusade, which was fought against the forces of the Muslim Saladin, the eponymous king, having been taken ill and needing meat for his restitution to health, is given the flesh of a young Saracen. The king is quickly restored to health after this. But it is by no means a crime confined to an uncivilised, distant past, for every so often a few new stories do surface. In 2014, eleven restaurant workers in Nigeria were arrested after the authorities discovered human heads in the refrigerator, which, it turns out, were sold as luxury delicacies to highly-valued customers. In 2009, a chef in California slow-cooked his wife and ate her. Sometimes cannibals have willing victims; in Germany in 2009, Armin Meiwes advertised on the internet for a well-built young man between 18 and 30 years old to be slaughtered and then consumed. A man named Bernd Jürgen Armando Brande volunteered, and when he arrived at Meiwes's house, Meiwes cut off Brande's penis, seasoned it, ate it, and allowed Brande to bleed to death. Miewes was able to live off the remainder of Brande's body for a full year before he was caught by the police. Ultimately, these types of stories play on people's deepest, darkest fears; we do not want to believe that there are individuals in society capable of carrying out such an act, but evidently such types do. And when new stories surface, the press is ever ready to sensationalise them and provide people with morbidly fascinating reading matter.

Chapter 7

Rob Roy: 'The Highland Rogue'

*It is not a romantic tale that the reader is here presented
with, but a real history: not the adventures of a Robinson
Crusoe, a Colonel Jack, or a Moll Flanders, but the actions
of a highland rogue; a man that has been so notorious to
pass for a mere imaginary person. North Britain has wanted
no proof of his existence; nor has his fame been unheard of in
England, and other parts of Europe.*

Anon. *The Highland Rogue* (1723)

*Rob Roy frequently saved his Grace the trouble of gathering
his rents; used to extort them from his tenants, and, at the
same time, gave them formal discharges ... [He] had his good
qualities; he spent his revenue generously; and, strange to
say, was a true friend to the widow and orphan.*

Anon. *The Edinburgh
Medley of Entertainment* (1800)

Rob Roy (1671-1734) was a Scottish outlaw who became a legend in his
own lifetime. While he was still alive, a pamphlet entitled *The Highland
Rogue; or, The Memorable Actions of the Celebrated Robert MacGregor*
(1723) was published which celebrated his life and deeds. It is an account
which, it has been theorised by early twentieth century scholars, might have
been written by Daniel Defoe, although it is not attributed to him by later
literary critics. *The Highland Rogue* also bears many similarities to an earlier
pamphlet entitled *The Scotch Rogue: or, The Life and Actions of Donald
MacDonald a Highland Scot* (1706). Given contemporary biographers'
propensity for plagiarism, we can assume that at least some of the material
for Rob Roy's life was adapted from that of MacDonald's. But it was Rob
Roy who made his mark in literature: after his death, Romantic poets and
novelists adapted his story, and he would appear as a highly romanticised

figure in late Victorian children's books and penny dreadfuls. Filmmakers would also, during the twentieth century, retell the story of Rob Roy, often named 'the Scottish Robin Hood'.

It is necessary first to examine the political context of the era in which Rob Roy and his family lived, for he participated in one of the largest rebellions against the Hanoverian monarchy in 1715. Charles I, of the Scottish House of Stuart, lost his head when he started a war with the parliament. In his place, Oliver Cromwell assumed the title of Lord Protector of the Commonwealth of England, Ireland, and Scotland. After Cromwell's death in 1658, the English elite invited Charles's son, who had been in exile in France, to resume the throne. The latter, known as the 'merry monarch', who was fond of partying and extravagances, represented a breath of fresh air for the English nation, in contrast to the austere, puritanical 'reign' of Cromwell. Charles II had a few disputes with parliament, but generally the relationship between the Crown and Parliament worked well.

However, Charles had a problem; he had produced no heir and the man due to succeed him, his brother James, had converted to Catholicism in 1668. This was a problem for the largely Protestant ruling elite in England, who viewed Catholics with intense suspicion. Indeed, we might say that English paranoia towards Catholicism is analogous to the 'Red Scare' in the USA during the Cold War era, when, under Senator Joseph McCarthy (1908–57), American citizens could find themselves being investigated for 'Un-American Activities' and Communist sympathies. Yet it appears that when Charles died in 1685, people were willing to give this Catholic monarch the benefit of the doubt, and James did try to be conciliatory to all people, even those who had sought to exclude him from the throne a few years earlier, but these cordial relations between James and Parliament were not to last. In the early part of his reign, he had to put down two rebellions; one led by the Earl of Argyll and another by the Duke of Monmouth. In order to shore up his power, James increased the size of his standing army. This worried many people because it appeared to be the same tactics that Cromwell had used to buttress his own position as a virtual dictator. He then began to promote Catholics to senior positions in government, and in 1687, through his attempted passage of the Declaration of Indulgence, began to advocate for the removal of laws which restricted the civil liberties of Catholics in Britain. The attempted passage of the Declaration again in 1688 proved to be too much for some of the Protestant nobles in England. Consequently, in June 1688, they invited James's Protestant son-in-law, William of Orange, who was married to James's daughter Mary, to invade England with an army and ascend the throne as joint monarchs. When William landed with his army, he faced little resistance, and because it was supposedly a bloodless coup d'état it has become known as 'the Glorious Revolution'. Of course, the Glorious Revolution was not without violence, and in 1689, Viscount Dundee led an army of Highland Clans against forces loyal to William III. The MacGregor clan supported this ultimately unsuccessful rising, with Rob Roy's father taking part in the Battle of Killicrankie, which proved to be a crushing defeat for the supporters of the Stuarts who called themselves Jacobites. Meantime, James fled to France where he was received by Louis XIV of France, and granted the use of a palace and a pension, until he died in 1701.

Let us now look at the life of Rob Roy himself. The author of *The Highland Rogue* begins his history by recounting the deeds of Rob Roy's ancestors. His forebears are portrayed as villainous brutes who were constantly in trouble with the law. For example, it is said that the MacGregor clan, 'liv'd by rapine, and made murder their diversion; and, in a word, they seem'd emulous to monopolize all that was wicked.'[75] The most notorious crime committed by the MacGregor clan is supposed to have occurred at some point during the seventeenth century. For reasons unknown, a dispute had arisen between the MacGregors and the family of Sir John Colquhoun (1596-1647). A later Victorian author, in *The Chiefs of Colquhoun* (1869), suspects that the reason for the dispute between the two families came about as a result of the King of Scotland having bestowed a military commission upon the Colquhouns. A modern historian of the Colquhoun clan puts a different case forward, arguing that the dispute between the two families arose as a consequence of the MacGregors having stolen livestock from the Colquhouns. Whatever the reasons for the dispute were, the imagination of the author of *The Highland Rogue* goes into overdrive, and says that one night, the MacGregors broke into the Colquhoun family's dwelling and massacred virtually the whole of the family, for which all of the MacGregors were outlawed.[76] We need not take this incident too seriously. That the MacGregor clan were once outlaws is beyond doubt, but the author has probably inserted the massacre for two reasons; to show that criminality ran through the MacGregor family from time immemorial, and to illustrate this he has probably drawn upon the memory of the Glencoe Massacre in 1692 to colour his account of the family's alleged criminality.

Rob Roy was born in Glengyle, near Stirling, and, due to the family's reputation as brigands, took his mother's name of Campbell. Unusually for a criminal biography, *The Highland Rogues* gives a moderately detailed description of what Rob Roy looked like when he was in his prime:

'He is a man of such prodigious strength, and of such an uncommon stature, the he approacheth even to a gigantic size: he wears a beard above a foot long, and not only his face, but his whole body, is covered with red hair, which is the reason he is probably called Rob-Roy, for that (in the highland dialect) signifies Red Robert.'[77]

Where the author of *The Highland Rogue* obtained this description of Rob Roy's appearance is unknown, but it has to be remembered that it was written for an English audience, printed in London. This is why we see a subtle sneering at the supposedly wild and savage men of the highlands, and furthermore Rob Roy's rustic dress would have been different to the allegedly civilised and refined clothing of English gentlemen in the early eighteenth century. The inhabitants of Scotland, were often unsympathetically stereotyped in the eighteenth century popular press, especially in satirical prints. For example, Charles Mosley's *Sawney in the Bog House* (c.1745) depicts an uneducated Scotsman, newly arrived in England, struggling to master the use of an English lavatory, and the print was later reissued by the popular artist James Gillray in 1779. Another unpleasant print from the latter part of the century entitled *The Flowers of Edinburgh* (1781) shows a highlander emptying his bowels into a bucket in the street, while from the house above him a maid empties a chamber pot out of the window.

In spite of the negative depictions of Scots, particularly Highland Scots, as brutish and uneducated, the young Rob Roy had, at first, what seemed to be a shrewd head for business. Having been brought up to the trade of a grazier, he set up his own business which went rather well in its early years. He also ingratiated himself with several of the local commercial and farming magnates. The result was that all the local people grew very fond of him. The proceeds from his trade as a grazier, as well as payments for protecting travellers as they travelled through the country, meant that his business grew. The 'protection' that he and his men offered travellers, however, was essentially a protection racket. Law enforcement in urban areas of England at this time was inadequate and marked by corruption. In early eighteenth century Scotland it was practically non-existent, and the job of being watchmen was often outsourced to the highland clans. And it could be lucrative; William Farquharson received £5,000 in just one year, 1653, from the gentry of Angus to protect their estates. To expand his commercial interests even more, Rob Roy took out a large amount of credit. Initially there were no problems, and he was repaying his creditors in accordance with the terms of his agreements with them. However, in 1712, a dispute over land arose between Rob Roy and one of his creditors, the Duke of Montrose, and the matter was referred to court. Montrose won the case, and then Rob Roy's other creditors began to call in their debts all at once. He pleaded with his creditors for more time to pay but it was to no avail. He, therefore, decided to give his creditors the slip and with his immediate and extended family, absconded to Glen Shira, under the protection of his friend, the Duke of Argyle. Having spent some time here, he then moved his forces to Craigrostan in the Highlands, near Loch Lomond. This was the perfect hideaway for a man who, to all intents and purposes, was now an outlaw:

> '[Craigrostan] is situated … on the borders of Lochlomond, and inviron'd with stupendous high mountains, and rocks of prodigious magnitude … 'tis a place of such strength and safety that one person, well-acquainted with it, and supplied with ammunition, might easily destroy an entire army.'[78]

Finding himself in this situation, he vowed vengeance on the Duke of Montrose. The place that he had chosen as a hideaway for him and his men was also situated perfectly between the lands of the Colquhoun family, the MacGregors' historic enemies, and that of Montrose.

The number of men that accompanied Rob Roy into his highland hideaway was considerable, and having no other means of support, they took to highway robbery to support themselves. The principal means through which they raised money, however, was through kidnapping people and collecting a ransom. As news of Rob Roy's exploits began to spread, we see typical 'good outlaw' scenarios attributed to him and his men. *The Highland Rogue* records one example in which the brigands kidnapped a gentleman. Upon learning that the man was in dire straits financially, Rob Roy set him free, and bestowed upon him a large amount of money, gave him a boat to make his travels easier, and even allowed one of his men, probably one of the younger MacGregors, to accompany the gentleman on the remainder of his journey as his servant. While Rob Roy was never famous for cruelty, the insertion of this episode into his biography is most likely a hangover from earlier outlaw narratives; Robin Hood in *A Gest of Robyn Hode* also helps a poor knight, gives him money, and sends Little John on a journey with the knight to act as his servant. Like all good outlaws, furthermore, Rob Roy is said to have stolen from the rich and redistributed his wealth among the poor.

Rob Roy and his men became ever daring in their exploits, and against the Duke of Montrose:

> 'disposed himself to employ every means of annoyance in his power [...conducting] nothing short of a predatory war against the Duke of Montrose, whom he considered to be the author of his exclusion from civil society.'[79]

The Duke was a rich man, with a vast amount of land whose tenants paid him rent. So the outlaws decided to hurt Montrose where it would hurt the most; in his pocket. Rob Roy received intelligence of the day when John Graham, the man who managed the finances on the duke's estate, would be journeying around the duke's lands collecting rents. As Graham was collecting rent from a tenant one evening, Rob Roy and the rest of the brigands surrounded the house. They entered and took from Graham £500, and in order to obtain more money, they kidnapped and ransomed him. Not being satisfied with taking a considerable amount of the duke's revenue, they soon after broke into his house, 'from whence (tho' not without opposition) they carry'd away a considerable prize.'[80]

Political upheavals in the early part of the eighteenth century provided Rob Roy with the perfect opportunity to wreak havoc against the establishment. As part of William and Mary's contract with Parliament, they had to agree to the Bill of Rights, which essentially affirmed the supremacy of Parliament over the Crown. One of the last important Acts passed by Parliament during William's reign was the Act of Settlement, which decreed that the Crowns of England and Ireland could only pass to non-Catholic heirs. After the deaths of Mary and William, the throne then passed to another member of the Stuart line, Anne, who reigned between 1702 and 1714. Anne, as Charles II, James II, William and Mary before her, was essentially the monarch of three nations; England, Scotland, and Ireland. The Act of Settlement did not yet apply to Scotland. Thus, one of Anne's pet projects was the creation of a political union between England and Scotland. After some fraught negotiations, which began in 1703, the two kingdoms of England and Scotland were finally united into a single political entity, the Kingdom of Great Britain in 1707. However, Anne, in spite of having been pregnant 17 times, died leaving no heir due to the various complications in the pregnancies. Thus, the throne of the newly-united kingdom passed over fifty possible Catholic heirs and settled upon George of Hanover, who ascended the throne as George I in 1714.

The new foreign king received a lukewarm reception in Britain. He could not even speak English, and riots accompanied the news of his coronation in many parts of Britain. It was not only the people at large who resented the new king, but also many of the ruling elite. Some high-ranking Tories at this time convinced James Francis Edward Stuart, the son of James II, that it would be a good idea for him to invade Britain. Once people saw the heir of the 'true' dynasty returned, they would surely flock to him, so it was reasoned. And in 1715, he invaded, and many people, particularly in Scotland, flocked to his standard. Like his father before him, Rob Roy lent his and his clan's support to the returned Stuart King, although it is likely that Rob Roy's support for the cause stemmed more from a desire to be a menace to the establishment, rather than a whole-hearted belief in the right of the Stuarts to reclaim the throne. Indeed, the MacGregor clan's contribution to the Jacobite war effort did not have any significant effect, and mostly the tales that are told of Rob Roy's exploits at this time were probably more of an irritant to the Hanoverians. During the early days of the rebellion, for instance, it is said that the MacGregors stole a number of boats belonging to the Hanoverian forces, taking them back to Craigrostan. But when the Hanoverian soldiers made an excursion there to recover the boats, the MacGregors, judging the situation and the superior number of the Hanoverians, decided not to put a fight and allowed the soldiers to take the boats back.

Having been pursued by the Hanoverians, Rob Roy thought fit to take himself and his men to the see the Earl of Mar at Perth, where he and his army were encamped, the Earl of Mar being one of the leading figures on the Stuart side in the Jacobite Rebellion of 1715. Mar asked Rob Roy to travel to Aberdeen to convince the other MacGregors living there to join the Jacobite standard as well. Yet when Rob Roy arrived, he found his remaining family there to be altogether gentrified. He chanced to meet with a distant relative named James Gregory, a doctor of science and literature. Although they had never met, Rob Roy and his estranged relative instantly became good friends, and later in life Rob Roy would return to see him.

After a cordial few days, Rob Roy and his men made their way back to the Earl of Mar. Rob Roy's support for the Jacobite cause was always lukewarm.

Moreover, his friend, the Duke of Argyle (1680-1743), was the leader of the government's army in Scotland. When push came to shove, Rob Roy was reluctant to serve in any army that opposed Argyle's. Thus, at the Battle of Sheriffmuir, on 13 November 1715, when called upon by the Earl of Mar to serve, Rob Roy flatly refused. When he received Mar's orders to join the attack, he is famously said to have told the messenger that he would not fight, '[for] if they cannot do without me, they cannot do it with me.' The battle proved to be a strategic victory for the Hanoverian government, and after the battle Rob Roy allowed his fellow outlaws to enrich themselves by plundering the possessions of dead soldiers. Walter Scott, who wrote the novel *Rob Roy* (1818), records that the brigand's neutrality on this occasion gave rise to a Scottish ballad:

> 'Rob Roy he stood watch
> On a hill for to catch
> The booty, for aught that I saw, man;
> For he ne'er advanced
> From the place where he stanced,
> Till nae mair was to do there at a' man.'

Ultimately, his neutrality did him no favours. After the Jacobite defeat, the Hanoverian government enacted some bitter recriminations against Jacobite supporters through the Act of Attainder. The rebels were deemed to be traitors, their properties were confiscated, and some of them were shipped off to America to serve as indentured labourers. Rob Roy and his followers were just some of the many people whose lives and properties were proscribed by these Acts. He subsequently returned to Craigrostan, where he continued his feud with the Duke of Montrose. In November 1716, the outlaws relieved the duke of over £300. John Graham was sent by Montrose to Chapel Errock, where all of the duke's tenants had been summoned, to collect the rents that they owed. The bandits burst into the house where the people were congregated and took all of the money. Rob Roy then had the audacity to write Montrose a receipt for it. At another point, Montrose decided it would be better to provide all of his tenants with guns, so that they might defend themselves against the marauders, but the MacGregor gang simply stole the guns. In addition, as much of Montrose's rents were paid in kind, he had built up considerable stores of grain. So the outlaws simply robbed the duke's granaries, but Rob Roy always made sure to leave a receipt for the duke so he knew who had taken them. The duke made several attempts to have the outlaw and his men arrested, and at one point in 1716, three parties of soldiers were sent into the Highlands to arrest him. However, it was to no avail, for the brigand always seemed to be one step ahead of the authorities for two reasons; his hideout was in a secluded part of the Highlands, an area which Rob Roy knew well but his pursuers did not, and his generosity to the poor ensured that he received regular intelligence about the movements of soldiers.

However, Rob Roy could not indefinitely evade the law. Walter Scott, in the preface to a later edition of *Rob Roy*, recalls conversing with an innkeeper who told him the story of the time that Montrose surprised and arrested the outlaw while travelling in the highlands with a party of armed men. Rob Roy's hands were tied and he was placed under guard at the back of the party, while Montrose led the way hoping to find somewhere secure in which to place his prisoner for the evening. The man guarding the outlaw, however, was an old acquaintance of Rob Roy's named James Stewart, and the brigand asked him to help him escape. His old friend came through for him, and allowed Rob Roy to give Montrose the slip. When Montrose learnt what had happened he was so enraged that he struck Stewart on the head with the butt of his pistol. After this, he continued the same mode of life that he had always followed, namely, being an irritant to the Duke of Montrose. News of Rob Roy's exploits spread as far as London, and in 1723, *The Highland Rogue* appeared in print. Rob Roy's name was thus added to the pantheon of criminals whose lives were immortalised in print during the early eighteenth century.

In 1725, General Wade was authorised by the British government to go to Scotland and offer amnesties to remaining Jacobite supporters, provided they wrote a letter expressing their desire to submit to the rule of George I. In his letter, Rob Roy said that he never even wanted to join the Jacobites, and that he would have backed the House of Hanover had it not been for the Duke of Montrose, who would surely have thrown him in gaol for debt. As further evidence of his loyalty to the Hanoverians, Rob Roy cited the time when he refused to attack the Duke of Argyle's forces. Whether Wade truly believed what was written in the letter is unclear, but it was best to stop the brigand being an annoyance to the country, and in October of the same year he received a formal pardon. As a show of good faith, he provided Wade with intelligence of Jacobite activities in the area, which led to the arrest of one man. And by the time of his pardon he was no longer in debt to the Duke of Montrose, for one of Rob Roy's punishments for his involvement in the 1715 was the confiscation of his property, which was then divided up among his creditors, with Montrose receiving the lion's share. Thus, he was free to live peacefully in his old age.

Rob Roy spent his last years living at Balquhidder. Scott ascribes a very romantic end to his life. While on his deathbed, he is said by Scott to have expressed regret for his criminal course of life. And upon learning that a local clansman, one of the MacLarens, with whom he was in a financial dispute with intended to visit him, he rose from the bed and donned his tartan. He had a short and civil conversation with the man. After this he said to his wife, "ha til mi tulidh" (we return no more), after which he died. He was laid to rest in Balquhidder churchyard.

It did not take long for legends to form around Rob Roy, and his grave became a pilgrimage site for tourists and Romantic poets such as William Wordsworth (1770-1850). However, the brigand found posthumous fame in Scott's *Rob Roy*. The principal protagonist of Scott's work is a man called Frank Osbaldistone who travels to Scotland to save his father's business, as he has had to go into hiding because of his Jacobite sympathies. Along the way, he meets Rob Roy and the outlaws. With the Jacobite threat having vanished by the time that Scott was writing, in the novel, Rob Roy is a romanticised freedom fighter wholeheartedly supporting Jacobite cause, even though, as we have seen, his dedication to the cause was a matter of convenience rather than a firm ideological belief. Scott's novel was retold in several plays throughout the country during the early nineteenth century. As a result of Scott's novel, Rob Roy appears as the hero of several late-Victorian and Edwardian penny dreadfuls, under the title of the *Rob Roy Library*. He is also the hero of some children's books, such as Gordon Stables's *Rob Roy MacGregor* (1902).

The twentieth century has witnessed three movie portrayals of Rob Roy's life story; the silent *Rob Roy* appeared in 1922. The title character was played by one of the stars of the silent movie age, David Hawthorne (1888-1942). Disney produced *Rob Roy: The Highland Rogue* (1953). The latter did not perform well in terms of box office receipts, and it is said to be one of the reasons why Disney refrained for a while from producing live-action costume dramas. One criticism of the novel in the *New York Times* was that the director, Harold French,

> 'based his script more on unfortified legend than on the novel of Sir Walter Scott [...he] has shaped his story from sheer acts of derring-do, and stretched out on a fuzzy line of conflict between the outlaw clan chieftain and the Crown. And it is strictly for bold and brawny action that Harold French has directed the film.'[81]

For this reviewer, if one wants to view a decent version of Rob Roy's story, then they should turn to Walter Scott. More successful was *Rob Roy* (1995) starring Liam Neeson in the title role. This last production has little relation to Scott's novel, and while it contains his personal rivalry against the Duke of Montrose, it does not include anything about his support for the Jacobite cause.

Rob Roy, largely as a result of Scott's novel, has remained a popular figure in Scotland. While his fame has not yet reached the same heights as that of the English Robin Hood, the two figures are often compared to each other. Rob Roy's grave even became a sight of pilgrimage for some of Scott's fellow Romantic poets, in particular William Wordsworth who, in 1803, inspired by the bravery of the man, wrote the following lines:

> *A famous man is Robin Hood,*
> *The English ballad-singer's joy!*
> *And Scotland has a thief as good,*
> *An outlaw of as daring mood;*
> *She has her brave ROB ROY!*
> *Then clear the weeds from off his Grave,*
> *And let us chant a passing stave,*
> *In honour of that Hero brave!*

Chapter 8

Jack Sheppard: The Original 'Jack the Lad'

Nor could any so handily break a lock,
As Sheppard, who stood on Newgate dock,
And nicknamed the gaolers around him "his flock!"
Which nobody can deny.

William Harrison Ainsworth,
Rookwood (1834)

Thornhill, 'tis thine to gild with fame,
Th' obscure, and raise the humble name;
To make form elude the grave,
And Sheppard from oblivion save.

Though life, in vain, the wretch implores,
An exile to the farthest shores;
Thy pencil brings a kind reprieve,
And bids the dying robber live.

This piece to latest times shall stand,
And show the wonders of thy hand;
Thus former masters graced their name,
And gave egregious robbers fame.

Apelles Alexander drew;
Caesar is to Aurelius due;
Cromwell in Lilly's work doth shine,
And Sheppard, Thornhill, lives in thine.

Anon. *Stanzas on the Portrait of*
Jack Sheppard (1840)

Jack Sheppard (1702-24) was one of eighteenth century London's most notorious thieves, an idle apprentice who cast aside his trade of a carpenter and took up a criminal career. Pamphlets published after his death celebrated his daring life and deeds, with his repeated escapes from gaol fuelling his fame and popularity. There are four sources which were published at the time which give an account of his life: *The History of the Remarkable Life of John Sheppard* (1724); *Authentic Memoirs of the Life and Surprising Adventures of John Sheppard* (1724); *A Narrative of all the Robberies, Escapes, &c. of John Sheppard* (1724); which was allegedly 'written by himself', although it was most likely written by Daniel Defoe, as well as the accounts we have preserved in *The Proceedings of the Old Bailey* and *The Ordinary of Newgate's Account*. Eventually he died an ignominious death at Tyburn, and it might be thought that he would be quickly forgotten. But he was not, for he was 'resurrected', so to speak, during the Victorian period when William Harrison Ainsworth published *Jack Sheppard* (1839). The novel caused a sensation, with press commentators denouncing it for encouraging unruly youths to follow a life of crime. Let us take a look at the life of the original 'Jack the lad'.[82]

Jack Sheppard was born in Stepney to a poor, destitute family. His father died when he was very young, and because his mother already had two children, with the father's absence she could not afford to feed another mouth on scant wages. The eldest child, Tom, was sent to be a servant in the family of a local lady. Young Jack was sent to the Bishopsgate workhouse to be raised and cared for under the parish authorities, while his sister sadly died in her infancy. Early eighteenth century workhouses were an altogether different type of institution to the cold and callous establishments which succeeded them in the Victorian era, after the passage of the Poor Law Amendment Act (1834). Paupers could come and go as they pleased, and they were actively encouraged to seek employment outside of the institution. They also functioned as emergency wards, causal night shelters, crèches, orphanages, alms houses and old people's homes. Workhouses were also the places to which paupers would go and collect their weekly pensions and 'outdoor relief' (a form of dole which was paid by the parish to those in need). According to the few accounts extant of life inside an eighteenth century workhouse, the paupers who found themselves reliant on parish support in these institutions were generally treated with kindness, and clothed and fed. Another function of the workhouse system at this time was to find work for young children, and place them as apprentices to small tradesmen. The Bishopsgate workhouse did this for young Jack Sheppard, who was bound as an apprentice carpenter on 2 April 1717 to Owen Wood, who lived in Wych Street. Life in a Georgian workhouse did get a little tougher following the introduction of The Workhouse Test Act (1723), whereupon paupers would have to prove that they deserved to receive poor relief, but at the time young Sheppard entered the system it would not have been in place.

Young Sheppard distinguished himself in the service of Wood and showed much potential. In the words of one account entitled *The History of the Remarkable Life of John Sheppard* (1724), as an apprentice Sheppard 'had a ready and ingenious hand, and soon became master of his business'.[83] His apprenticeship continued successfully for about six years until he met a prostitute named Elizabeth Lyon, alias Edgworth Bess, who is blamed by Sheppard's biographer for having induced him to follow a life of crime; in a heavily moralist tone that is characteristic of all eighteenth-century crime writing, we read, 'now was laid the foundation of his ruin!'[84] Sheppard appears to have become a bit of a party animal after his meeting with Bess, for his biography records that what next ensued was a neglect of duty, both to God and his master, and staying out all night in public houses. Accordingly, in order to try and teach him not to stay out drinking, Wood tried locking him out one night. But Sheppard was adept at picking locks, and oftentimes Mr. Wood would wake up on a morning to find Sheppard in the house in spite of shutting him out.

Wood must have been a kind-hearted gentleman, for it is a wonder that he did not simply dismiss Sheppard for his unruliness. He was sent to carry out a repair at the house of a tailor, Bain. While in attendance at the latter's house, Sheppard committed his first robbery. He stole twenty-four yards of fustian, although he had difficulty in finding a purchaser for it, so he kept it hidden in a trunk. Sheppard then returned to Bain's at night a few days later, picked the lock on the front door, and helped himself to £7 in cash as well as other goods to the value of £14. Wood and Bain were unaware that it was Sheppard who had stolen the goods, and Bain's lodger was suspected of stealing them instead. Sheppard only confessed this first crime as he was awaiting execution in gaol.

Eventually, Sheppard's continued unruliness meant that enough was enough for Wood, and he and Sheppard finally parted ways. He was now exposed, in the words of one biographer, to all of the temptations that early Georgian London had to offer. At this point he also became acquainted with a variety of figures from the eighteenth century criminal underworld such as Joseph 'Blueskin' Blake, William Field, and James Sykes *alias* Hell and

Fury. Sheppard did manage to secure some causal employment with another carpenter named Charles. However it seemed that he could not keep himself from stealing, for one day, Charles sent Sheppard to carry out some repairs at a customer's house. While on this job he stole £7 10s, some silverware, six gold rings, as well as a considerable quantity of linen. He was never arrested for this, however, and only confessed this to his biographer while awaiting his execution in prison.

We do not know the details of what Jack Sheppard's relationship with his brother, Thomas, was like but we can surmise that they did not feel a sense of familial loyalty to each other. In February 1724, Thomas was in Newgate for having burgled and stolen from the house of a linen draper named Mary Cook goods to the value of £60. Perhaps in return for leniency in his sentence, he turned King's Evidence and accused Jack and Bess of having been his accomplices in the robbery. As London did not at this time have a professional police force, with law enforcement left to part time constables and night watchmen, as well as thief takers, it made sense for the authorities to convince criminals to turn on their accomplices. Thus, a warrant was drawn up for Jack and Bess, with a reward offered for their capture.

Clearly there was no such thing as honour among thieves in Sheppard's criminal network, because it was one of his fellow robbers, James Sykes, who decided to betray him at the behest of Jonathan Wild (c. 1682-1725), the self-styled 'Thief Taker General of Great Britain'. Consequently, Sykes invited Sheppard one night to a tavern in Seven Dials to play a game of skittles. At this time, Seven Dials was a crime-ridden rookery. Considered a 'no go' area for respectable men and women, it was a place where a person could enjoy sex, gambling and low theatre, in addition to being a place where thieves could meet and plot their next robberies. Sheppard arrived and commenced began playing a game with Sykes and some of the other dubious characters present. As the night wore on, Sykes sent a letter to the local constable, Mr. Price. Sheppard was considerably drunk when Price arrived to arrest him, so he was probably unable to even make an effective escape. Sheppard was then taken before Justice Pary to be arraigned. It was much too late in the evening for the justice to do anything with the youth, so he ordered that Sheppard be confined in the St. Giles' roundhouse until he could be examined the next day. The roundhouse was a small village lock-up in which offenders were detained for a day or two. People were often detained for being drunk and disorderly or some other minor misdemeanour. Young Sheppard did not plan on staying very long here, however; he broke through the roof and climbed out of it and having tied a sheet and blanket together, he simply lowered himself down to the ground and set himself free.

As we will see shortly, Sheppard was indeed very good at escaping from gaol. However, he was not particularly adept at evading recapture once he had escaped. On 19 May 1724, Sheppard and one of his associates named Benson were walking through Leicester Fields (present-day Leicester Square), and the former decided to rob a gentleman of his watch. Sheppard was seen by a passer-by, however, and a hue-and-cry was raised. There were various forms of hue-and-cry. If one witnessed a robbery in the street, one might shout 'stop thief!' whereupon good citizens nearby were obliged, as part of their civic duty, to pursue the thief. The hue-and-cry could also be carried out in a more organised manner, however; for example, a victim of a crime could go to the local constable and tell him that he or she had had something stolen. The constable would then summon the men of the town to hunt down the offender. In Sheppard's case, it was the first type of hue-and-cry, for his biography tells us that he took to his heels, but ultimately to no avail as he was eventually apprehended by a constable and conveyed to St. Ann's roundhouse in Soho where he was secured until the next morning. During his confinement, Bess also came to see him but when the guard learned who she was she was apprehended as well. Sheppard did not manage to escape from the roundhouse in Soho but was taken before a magistrate, and thereafter he and Bess were confined in the same cell at the New Prison at Clerkenwell. Having heard of his recent escape from the roundhouse in St. Giles, Sheppard was confined in the cell with a ball and chain on one of his legs.

During the eighteenth century, prisons were still far from the large penal institutions that they were to become in the nineteenth century. They were privately run, profit making institutions. Although prisoners were confined, their experience and level of comfort in gaol largely depended upon how rich they were. There is a scene that neatly illustrates this in *The Beggar's Opera*. In the play, the highwayman Captain Macheath, having been taken to Newgate, asks the gaoler Lockit for some comfortable manacles. In order to procure them, the captain must pay garnish:

> '*Lockit*. Noble Captain, you are welcome, You have not been
> a lodger of mine this year and a half. You know the custom,
> Captain, garnish. Hand me down those fetters there.

'*Macheath*. Those, Mr. Lockit, seem to be the heaviest of the whole set. With your leave, I should like the further pair better.

'*Lock*. Look ye, Captain, we know what is fittest for our prisoners. When a gentleman uses me with civility, I always do the best I can to please him – hand them down I say – We have them of all prices, from one guinea to ten, and 'tis fitting every gentleman should please himself.

'*Mach*. I understand you, Sir. *[Gives money.]* The fees here are so many and so exorbitant, that few fortunes can bear the expence [sic] of getting off handsomely or dying like a gentleman.'[85]

Macheath in Gay's opera was based in part upon Sheppard. Wealthier prisoners could pay for their own furnished private cells, while poorer prisoners languished in the pit, where disease was rife. Gaol-keepers were under no obligation to provide food to prisoners, which often meant that those in the lower part of the gaol had to beg for alms to those outside the prison. In contrast, prisoners with money could dine on fine food and drink. There were also no limits on visiting times in eighteenth-century prisons, and all prisoners were entitled to have visitors who often brought them food and drink.

Judging by the following episode in Jack Sheppard's biography, it seems that visitors were rarely, if ever, thoroughly searched upon entering prison as they are now. One of Sheppard's visitors secreted some tools for him to use in his cell, and in the course of a few days he eventually sawed off his fetters. Then one night, he sawed through some of the iron bars in the window and, attaching a blanket and sheet to one of the remaining bars, he and Bess climbed through the window and lowered themselves to the ground. As it happens, their cell overlooked the courtyard of another prison, the Clerkenwell Bridewell. This was no obstacle to the nimble young thief and his missus, however, for with gimlets and pincers at the ready they scaled the walls and climbed over it, and set themselves at liberty. News of this latest escape caused something of a sensation in the press and, if contemporary accounts are to be believed, the broken bars and the sheet that was tied together to effect the escape were preserved as a tourist attraction for visitors to the prison in the weeks and months after Sheppard's death.

Perhaps the most prudent thing that Sheppard could have done at this point would have been to leave London and set up a new life in the country.

But his biography tells us that, 'Sheppard, not warned by this admonition, returns [to a life of crime] like a dog to his vomit'. His criminal activities are depicted in contemporary reports as though they were an addiction from which it was hard for him to break free. For example, in Charles Johnson's *Lives of the Most Remarkable Criminals* (1735), we are told that a robber named Robert Crouch, addicted to gaming, whoring, and drinking. These vices are responsible for his descent into crime, and Johnson tells us that another robber called Arthur Chambers was, from his youth, addicted to robbing and pilfering. Sheppard subsequently returned to the area near Wych Street, close to where Mr. Wood lived, and began plotting another robbery with an apprentice named Anthony Lamb, to rob the possessions of a tailor named Barton, who lodged at the house of Henry Carter, a manufacturer of mathematical instruments. Lamb was Carter's apprentice, and one night he let Sheppard and another felon named Charles Grace into the house when everyone was asleep. Creeping up to Barton's bedroom, Sheppard and Grace entered it. The latter stood by Barton's bedside with a loaded pistol to shoot him in the head if he woke up. Luckily for Barton he did not, as he had been on a night out at the local tavern with friends that night, and was sleeping soundly because of the drink. Meantime, Sheppard was busy opening the locks of the trunks in the room, and eventually he managed to take goods and cash that amounted to about £300, a sizeable sum during the eighteenth century. The goods were then sold to a fence in Lewkenor's Lane, which like Seven Dials was another place that was noted for its criminality. Contemporary accounts do not tell us why Lamb was suspected by his master, but he was, and he was taken before Justice Newton. At his trial on 8 July 1724, Lamb made a full confession, and the judge in this case being disposed to show leniency, instead of receiving the death sentence Lamb was transported.[86]

During his confinement in late June 1724, Lamb must have told his father of another robbery that Sheppard was planning to commit at the house of a woollen-draper in the Strand called Kneebone. Thanks to Lamb's information, Kneebone and his servants were ready for Sheppard and his accomplices. Jack and his gang must have realised that something was up, for as they tried picking the lock on Kneebone's front door one of the maids heard Jack say, 'Damn him; if [we can't] enter that night they would have another, and have three hundred pounds.' And so the enterprise was abandoned by Sheppard and his crew until the evening of 19 July when, in concert with Joseph Blueskin Blake, Jack and the gang broke into Kneebone's cellar while the household were asleep and they stole one hundred and eighty yards of woollen cloth, a beaver hat, a pair of silver spoons, a handkerchief and a penknife, the total value of which was about £50.

Sheppard was not only a mere burglar but also turned his hand to highway robbery. On 19 July, he and Blueskin robbed the coach of a lady travelling on Hampstead Road of all of her money, with her footman being no match for Sheppard and his gang in a fight. Further highway robberies followed throughout the July and August. In the meantime, Kneebone applied to Jonathan Wild to affect the return of his stolen goods. Wild knew how to get to Sheppard, and accordingly he approached Bess in a tavern near Temple Bar, and he must have threatened her because she told him where Sheppard was hiding out. The next day he was arrested at Blueskin's mother's house by a man named Quilt, who was one of Wild's henchmen. After a scuffle in which Sheppard pointed a loaded pistol at Quilt, he was taken before the magistrate and indicted upon several counts of robbery. The death sentence was pronounced upon him, in spite of Sheppard's pleas for mercy on account of his youth.

Sheppard was taken back to gaol to await his execution. He would not stay there long, however; Bess had already been released from prison, and shortly before his execution she went to visit Sheppard in the condemned hold. He had already procured some instruments to pick the locks on his fetters, and while Bess was with him in the cell Sheppard began to work on setting himself free of his irons. Having done this, he then dressed up in women's clothes, which had probably been brought to him by Bess, and simply walked past the turnkeys and out of the prison (the door to the cell which housed Jack Sheppard can be seen in the gardens of Newby Hall in North Yorkshire). Once at liberty, Sheppard and Bess made the wise decision of retiring to the country to the house of some acquaintances in Warden, Northamptonshire where he stayed for the best part of a week, under the assumed identity of a butcher. His escape caused a sensation in the press and London society, with everyone's curiosity stoked about the boy who had escaped from gaol not once, not twice, but three times thus far.

Sheppard and Bess returned to London on 8 September, and went to a tavern. Their refreshments were cut short, however, when another man thought he recognised him, so the pair made a quick exit. At about eight o'clock in the evening, Sheppard passed a watchmaker's shop that was seemingly unattended except by a young apprentice boy. Sheppard then went round the back of the shop, broke open the door, and stole three silver watches which were valued at £15. Over the next few days, as a result of several sightings, news spread around London that Sheppard had returned to his old haunts. People such as Mr Kneebone were in fear for their lives, and several shopkeepers in the area of Wych Street and Drury Lane spent a lot of money fortifying their premises from potential burglaries.

Meantime, the Newgate turnkeys, who had received a great deal of public censure for Sheppard's previous escape (some people had even accused them of taking bribes from Sheppard), resolved to hunt the escaped felon down. Sheppard's biography records that the gaol-keepers spared no expense in order to bring Sheppard to justice. One of the turnkeys, Langley, saw Sheppard and an accomplice of his named Page disguised as butchers. Langley pointed his pistol at Page who immediately surrendered himself, but the 'slippery eel' Sheppard, darted off and took refuge in the stable of a farmhouse. The 'Newgate cavalry' was close on his heels, however, and the gaolers discovered and apprehended him. Sheppard appears to have been good-natured about the whole affair, and if contemporary accounts are to be believed, while the gaolers were waiting for a carriage to take him back to Newgate he drank brandy and exchanged jokes with them. When he arrived at Newgate, he did try cheekily making a run for it but was stopped by the gaolers.

When he was placed in gaol this time around, the keepers put a ball and chain on both legs. During his confinement, many members of the public came to view him, as the lad who had escaped from prison on multiple occasions was now a celebrity. His portrait was even painted by James Thornhill (c.1675-1734), who was father-in-law to the famous artist, William Hogarth (1697-1764). During this time, he was still plotting another escape, and in his cell one day the goal-keepers found a chisel, two files, and a hammer concealed in a Bible. The gaolers resolved to move him from the condemned hold to a place called the castle, located in the centre of the prison and from which it should have been impossible to escape, especially since the chains on his legs were now connected to two large iron staples in the wall. In this part of the prison he entertained many members of polite society, often sharing a drink with them and having a bit of banter:

'One Sunday ... the Lord Mayor ask'd a turnkey, *Which was Sheppard*, the man pointed to him. Says Sheppard, *yes sir, I am the Sheppard, and all the gaolers in the town are my flock, and I cannot stir into the country but they are all at my heels baughing after me.*'[87]

He seems also to have developed a good relationship with some of the turnkeys, despite being under sentence of death. However, one morning, as one of the gaolers was making his rounds, he stopped by Sheppard's cell and upon opening it found a pile of rubble; Sheppard had escaped again! Just as he had done before, Sheppard had broken into a number of other strong rooms in the castle, and then out of one of the cells had, by means of a blanket and a sheet tied together, lowered himself down on to the roofs of the dwellings below. The escape sent the gaolers into a frenzy, while news of Sheppard's latest daring exploit caused an even greater public sensation, with people visiting Newgate specially to see the damage he had caused. The authorities at the time were not even sure how exactly he had escaped, and so miraculous did the escape seem that some of the turnkeys surmised that the devil must have come to Sheppard in the night and helped him.

Young Sheppard was not to be at liberty for long, however, and he was soon retaken by a bailiff named Ireton. During his final period of confinement, all of his thoughts were taken up with devising a possible escape. Even as he was being taken to Tyburn, officials found a file on his person. Hopes of escape proved to be rather forlorn; on 16 November 1724, Sheppard was hanged by the neck. It took approximately fifteen minutes for him to die, due to the slightness of his body, which had served him so well in his many escapes.

The memory of Jack Sheppard refused to die, however, and his life story was reprinted in the works of Charles Johnson, as well as several other eighteenth-century true crime books such as *The Newgate Calendar*. However, over a century after he died, Jack Sheppard would again become infamous in William Harrison Ainsworth's immensely popular 'Newgate novel' entitled *Jack Sheppard: A Romance* (1839). In the novel, Jack is portrayed as a well-meaning young lad who, as a result of the machinations of Jonathan Wild, is sucked into the eighteenth century criminal underworld. The scenes of his escapes from prison were exciting and brought to vivid life by the illustrator, George Cruikshank. And the novel soon became a 'multimedia' event; there were eight concurrently-running theatre shows in London's West End featuring Sheppard's story, as well as street shows, pamphlets, and souvenirs (apparently, theatre-goers could even purchase a bag of toy files and lock picks).

In spite of good reviews, Ainsworth's best-selling book (which even outsold Charles Dickens' *Oliver Twist* published the year before) came in for some criticism by Victorian reviewers. A review in *The Athenaeum*, for example, denounced *Jack Sheppard* as 'a bad book, and what is worse, one of a class of bad books, got up for a bad people...a history of vulgar and disgusting atrocities.'[88] Matters came to head in July 1840 when Lord William Russell was murdered in his sleep by his valet, Benjamin Courvoisier. In one of several public confessions, Courvoisier stated that the idea for murdering his master came from having read *Jack Sheppard.* This was enough for the press to latch on to; Ainsworth's novel was, in their eyes, capable of inducing impressionable people to commit the foulest of all crimes. Other writers lined up to denounce Ainsworth's work such as William Makepeace Thackeray who, in the preface to his novel *Catherine* (1840) criticised those who portrayed criminals as romantic figures, although he did not mention Ainsworth by name. Ainsworth responded to his critics by denouncing their attacks as nothing more than unfounded, 'virulent and libellous attack upon my romance.'[89] However, the damage had been done, and there was now a moral panic about the influence of the novel. This was because Jack Sheppard in Ainsworth's novel is unashamed of his criminality and glories in it. Moreover, there is no justification for Sheppard's crimes in the novel, for he is hardly a Robin Hood or a Rob Roy, fighting for a noble cause. In spite of his crimes, furthermore, Ainsworth's portrayal of Jack Sheppard presents him as neither wholly good nor wholly evil; while he is a thief, his heart is in the right place; he is loyal to his friends and his mother, Joan. And it is his devotion to his mother that leads to his arrest, for he is apprehended at her funeral by Jonathan Wild. It was the moral ambiguity of Sheppard's personality in the novel that accounts for why the novel was deemed to be truly subversive by middle-class moralists in the press; they objected to mixed motives and mixed morality, and preferred portrayals of life in which criminality was condemned outright rather than being simultaneously criticised and celebrated.

In spite of the condemnation of Ainsworth's novel, 'Sheppard-mania' continued throughout the nineteenth century. While Ainsworth's work was published in the expensive three volume format, to suit those with more modest incomes, Ainsworth's tale was virtually plagiarised by penny blood authors, many of whom chose to remain anonymous. Among these were: *The History of Jack Sheppard: His Wonderful Exploits and Escapes* (1839); *The Life of Jack Sheppard, the Housebreaker* (1840); *The Eventful Life and Unparalleled Exploits of the Notorious Jack Sheppard* (1840); *The Life and Adventures of Jack Sheppard* (1840); as well as Lincoln Fortescue's similarly titled *The Life and Adventures of Jack Sheppard* (1845); and *Jack Sheppard; or, London in the Last Century* (1847). There was also a thriving market for prints depicting Sheppard's escapes from gaol, as Henry Mayhew attests in *London Labour and the London Poor* (1851).

The fears and anxieties of the Victorian middle classes, regarding the supposed connection between criminality and the glorification of Jack Sheppard, did not go away. He appeared in a number of penny bloods in the latter half of the century, such as *Blueskin: A Romance of the Last Century* (1867); *Tom King and Jonathan Wild; or, the Days of Young Jack Sheppard* (1870); and *Jack Sheppard: His Real Life and Exploits* (1890). These were published in addition to shorter stories contained in boys' magazines such as *The Boys' Leisure Hour*, *The Boys of Britain*, *The Boys' Standard*, and *Famous Crimes*. The police, the courts, and the conservative press often attributed the rise of juvenile crime to the reading of such penny dreadfuls. For example, Samuel Phillips Day in *Juvenile Crime: Its Causes, Character, and Cure* (1858) argues that juvenile delinquency:

> '... arises from demoralising publications, the number of which, from the immense circulation they obtain, it is difficult to compute. One thing is certain, that they are fraught with great evil to the community. Under this head may particularly be mentioned the lives of notorious robbers and highwaymen, such as Jack Sheppard.'[90]

Henry Mayhew, reporting upon the state of the prison system in the 1860s, questioned a number of juvenile criminals about their reading matter, and Jack Sheppard was idolised by the boys:

> 'Respecting their education, according to the popular meaning of the term, 63 of the 150 were able to read and write, and they were principally thieves. 50 of this number said they had read *Jack Sheppard*, and the lives of Dick Turpin and Claude Du Val, and all the other popular thieves' novels, as well as the *Newgate Calendar*, and the lives of the robbers and pirates. Those who could not read themselves, said that *Jack Sheppard* was read out to them at the lodging houses. Numbers avowed that they had been induced to resort to an abandoned course of life from reading the lives of notorious thieves, and novels about highway robbers. When asked what they thought of Jack Sheppard, several bawled out – "He's a regular brick!" – a sentiment which was almost universally concurred in by

the deafening shouts and plaudits which followed. When questioned as to whether they would like to have been Jack Sheppard, the answer was, "Yes, if the times were the same now as they were then!"'[91]

At the trial of an eighteen-year-old burglar in 1877, the offender said that the whole of his criminal career 'was owing to reading books – the *Boys of England, Young Men of Great Britain*, and others…which included *Jack Sheppard*.'[92] Of course, debates about the supposed links between violent entertainment and juvenile delinquency still rage today. Granted, such entertainment can possibly incite youths with impressionable minds to commit atrocities, but journalists who stoke moral panics in the press can often be prone to exaggeration. This was a point recognised by G. K. Chesterton, who in an essay entitled 'In Defence of Penny Dreadfuls,' argued that much of the furore around these publications was unfounded, and a little bit hypocritical as well, given that a lot of 'high' literature also featured tales of thieves and robbers, as the literary critic and novelist, Arthur Quiller Couch, pointed out in 1901:

'There is no class of vulgar publications about which there is, to my mind, more utterly ridiculous exaggeration and misconception than the current boys' literature of the lowest stratum … Among these stories there are a certain number which deal sympathetically with the adventures of robbers, outlaws, and pirates, which present in a dignified and romantic light thieves and murderers like Dick Turpin and Claude Duval. That is to say, they do precisely the same thing as Scott's *Ivanhoe*, Scott's *Rob Roy*, Scott's *Lady of the Lake*, Byron's *Corsair*, Wordsworth's *Rob Roy's Grave*, Stevenson's *Macaire*, Mr. Max Pemberton's *Iron Pirate*, and a thousand more works distributed systematically as prizes and Christmas presents. Nobody imagines that an admiration of [Robin of] Locksley in *Ivanhoe* will lead a boy to shoot Japanese arrows at the deer in Richmond Park; no one thinks that the incautious opening of Wordsworth at the poem on Rob Roy will set him up for life as a blackmailer. In the case of our own class, we recognise that this wild life is contemplated with pleasure by the young, not because it is like their own life, but because it is different from it. It might at least cross our minds that, for whatever other reason the errand-boy reads *The Red Revenge*, it really is not because he is dripping with the gore of his own friends and relatives.'[93]

Quiller Couch had a point; Scott's *Ivanhoe* (1819) and *Rob Roy* (1818) celebrate the lives of outlaws, although nobody at the time would have thought of criticising Scott. But of course, the works of Scott were seen as quite 'middle class' pieces of literature, and must surely have been more respectable than the vulgar penny dreadfuls devoured by young lads.

During the twentieth century, Jack Sheppard's fame died down somewhat, and his story is known mainly now to historians of crime and eighteenth century history enthusiasts. There was a now little-known movie entitled *Where's Jack?* (1969), starring Tommy Steele as Jack Sheppard and Stanley Baker as Jonathan Wild. However, this appears to have been the last major reworking of the Jack Sheppard story. To conclude this account of Sheppard's life and 'literary afterlife', we can justifiably say that, had you lived during the eighteenth or nineteenth centuries, the name of Jack Sheppard would have been as familiar to you as that of Robin Hood.

Chapter 9

Jonathan Wild: London's First Mob Boss

As we are to record the actions of a great man, so we have
nowhere mentioned any spark of goodness, which had
discovered itself either faintly in him, or more glaringly
in any other person, but as a meanness and imperfection,
disqualifying them for undertakings which lead to honour
and esteem among men. As our hero had as little as, perhaps,
is to be found of that meanness, indeed enough only to make
him partaker of the imperfection of humanity, instead of
the perfections of diabolism, we have ventured to call him
"THE GREAT;" nor do we doubt that our reader, when he
hath perused his story, will concur with us in allowing him
that title.

> Henry Fielding, *The History of the
> Life of Jonathan Wild, the Great* (1743)

The history of the arts, deceptions, cruelty, and perfidy of
this man, have alone filled a volume; and, should he occupy
more room in our epitome than may be deemed necessary, we
have only to observe, that the whole catalogue of other crimes
exposed in this chronology, centred in one individual, would
scarcely produce a parallel with this thief-taker, and most
finished thief.

> *The New Newgate Calendar* (1824)

When people hear the term, 'organised crime', they usually think of
twentieth century criminal networks such as the Sicilian mafia, the
Russian mafia, the Chinese Triad, or the Japanese Yakuza. For most people,
rarely would the term conjure images from eighteenth-century England.

Yet sophisticated gangs of criminals did operate at this time; whether it was pirates, who can justifiably be classed as a form of early modern transnational organised crime, or the groups of banditti and highwaymen who terrorised the roads of England in the eighteenth century. For a short time in the early eighteenth century, however, all of the crime in London was controlled by one man. And it is to the first notable instance of organised crime in Britain that we now turn, as we delve into the life of the self-styled 'Thief Taker General of Britain and Ireland', Jonathan Wild (c. 1683-1725). He was London's chief agent of law enforcement, but he was also a master criminal.

Organised crime has always flourished in parts of the world where the state is unwilling or unable to maintain law and order. As we have seen in previous chapters, the state of law enforcement in the eighteenth century was not as professional as it is today. Before Henry Fielding established the Bow Street Runners in 1749, law enforcement in London was the duty of part time and often unpaid constables, who, if a criminal was caught, often had to be found 'red-handed'. Even after Fielding founded his runners, there were so few of them that they could never truly mount a serious assault on rising crime rates. It was a reactive system of policing, rather than a preventative one. Even if a felon was caught, it was the victim who had to pay the courts to prosecute the offender. If somebody found themselves the victim of a robbery, it was much easier for them to apply to their local thief taker. The thief taker would hold an interview with the victim and ascertain what had been stolen. The thief taker would then place an advertisement in the local paper, similar to the following example which Wild himself placed in *The Daily Courant* in 1715:

> 'Lost on Friday night last, a green vellum letter-case ... if the person who hath found this case and tickets, &c. will bring them to Mr. Jonathan Wild at the Old Bailey ... he shall have two guineas reward and no questions asked.'[94]

In such situations, the victim of the crime had their stolen goods returned to them and had bypassed an expensive prosecution in the courts (if indeed the thief could ever be found); the thief received a fee for the items he had stolen, and Wild was paid as well. The arrangement was beneficial for everybody. It was certainly a good arrangement for a man such as Jonathan Wild, who, unbeknownst to the general public, was actually directing virtually all of the criminal activity in London.

Jonathan Wild was born in Wolverhampton to honest and hardworking parents. Some later biographies do attempt to give a genealogy for Wild as far back as the sixteenth century, saying that he is descended from the Irish clan of Patrick Mac Judas Wild. However, this is almost certainly fictional; the reference to Judas in the name is meant to evoke images of Christ's betrayer, and it is doubtful that a poor family, at this point, could ever trace their 'pedigree', as the biographers call it, back to the time of Henry VIII.

As with many criminals, little is known of Wild's early life. Although his parents were poor, they ensured that Wild, along with his siblings, received an education. After his rudimentary schooling, he was apprenticed to a buckle maker in Birmingham. Apprenticeships usually lasted for seven years, the terms of which were laid down in the Statute of Artificers (1562). It was typically served in two stages; in the early years, the indentured boy worked for free while learning the trade; in the second half of the appointment he would repay his master's investment by working for below-the-market wages. Wild was evidently disappointed with low pay in the second half of his term because he absconded from his apprenticeship and became a servant in the household of a gentleman from Staffordshire. For some unknown reason, Wild was dismissed from service, and afterwards ventured back home to Wolverhampton to become his own boss, taking up the trade of a buckle-maker.

By all accounts, Wild's business in Wolverhampton was doing well, but he got bored with it and, abandoning his wife and children (contemporary accounts do not say when or to whom he was married), he travelled to London to ply his trade there. Business did not go well in the capital, however, and soon he found himself in the Wood Street Compter, imprisoned for debt; the notorious highwayman, James Hind, was also imprisoned here. The practice of sending debtors to prison lasted into the nineteenth century, and Charles Dickens, drawing upon his childhood experiences, wrote *Little Dorrit* (1855-57), which dealt directly with injustices of the debtors' prison system. Confinement in these institutions did not clear the debt, and before the debtor was released he or she had to pay their creditors in full. And those who found themselves in the Compter or, like Little Dorrit's father, in the Marshalsea, also had to pay for their board. But with no family or friends around him to help him out with food and other everyday expenses, Wild was placed in the paupers' part of it, where conditions were grim and food was meagre. Things eventually began looking up for Wild, however, and due to the fact that he proved to be a model prisoner, he was granted the 'liberty of the gate', which meant that he could leave the prison during the day time to seek work, as long as he returned on an evening. The gaol-keepers were so impressed with his good conduct that they employed him to work in the prison, where his principal duties were to work the night shift and ensure that new prisoners were entered into the system.

One night a woman named Mary Milliner came into the prison while Wild was on the night shift. It is not known why she came, for she does not appear to have been a prisoner. It is likely that she was a prostitute, and was coming to ply her trade in the gaol; prisoners at this time were permitted visitors. A friendship developed between Wild and Milliner, which soon progressed into a relationship. She then acquainted him with the gang of criminals which she used to run with, and taught Wild the art of conning people out of money. This training in the criminal arts served him well and he was soon able to pay off his creditors and gain his freedom. Once he was out, although Wild and Milliner were both married to other people, they pretended that they were husband and wife (one of his biographies records that he had a total of six unofficial wives). Through Milliner, Wild became acquainted with many more gangs from the London underworld, and Wild and Milliner commenced a criminal career by working in partnership as a buttock-and-file. There are many instances of men and women working this way in eighteenth-century London; the female 'buttock' would entice an unsuspecting passer-by down a dark alley with the offer of cheap sex, the male 'file' would then rob the victim, and perhaps give him a blow on the head for good measure.

Wild made himself useful to the thieves with which he became acquainted by acting as a receiver of stolen goods, and he eventually cornered the market in this respect with the result that thieves could not help but go through Wild to get rid of their stolen goods. There had been a decline in the number of prosecutions for people charged with receiving stolen goods. The 'profession' of receiving, for want of a better word, had been clamped down on by the government as the result of an Act of Parliament passed in 1699, which had made it a felony to knowingly receive stolen goods (prior to this, only aiding and abetting a thief was a crime, while the law regarding the handling of stolen goods was left vague). Yet even in this business, Wild showed himself to be a shrewd operator; he would never physically receive the stolen goods himself but rather, when a thief came to him with something, he would merely direct the robber where to store it until it could be safely sold. Thus, nothing could be pinned personally on to him.

To supplement his income from his new trade as a receiver of stolen goods, and to enhance his position in the criminal underworld, Wild became a thief taker. He began his career in the employ of Charles Hitchin (c.1675–1727). However, Wild moved to oust Hitchin from the profession altogether, and this was achieved by exposing the latter's corruption by colluding with thieves and rogues in various robberies in the press, and in the other pamphlets by insinuating that Hitchin was a homosexual. Hitchin hit back and a war of words in the press soon followed. However, by 1718, Hitchin was discredited in the public arena. It is at this point that Wild set himself up as 'Thief Taker General'.

Wild's rise to the top of the criminal underworld seemed complete, but he was acting as a law enforcer as well. While he was indeed directing many of the activities of many of the thieves under him, he had to show that he was doing his bit for the authorities. Consequently, every so often he would betray one of the thieves in his employ to the authorities, particularly if the reward for catching a thief was a substantial amount. For example, according to a later account of Wild's life, in 1716 a young gentleman and his mother were robbed in Grays-Inn-Gardens, London. The mother went to Wild to tell him what had been stolen and also gave a thorough description of the malefactors, and, according to the *Newgate Calendar*, 'Wild immediately judged the gang to be composed of William White, Thomas Turland, John Chapman alias Edward Darvel, Timothy Dun, and Isaac Rag.' While the men were drinking with their female companions in a tavern, Wild along with several other men appeared and arrested them all. In *The Beggar's Opera*, the hero, the highwayman Captain Macheath, was based upon Jack Sheppard and the villain of the story, Peachum, was based upon Jonathan Wild. The opening scene of the play sees Peachum, a fence and a thief taker, looking over his register of thieves to see who will live, and who will die:

> '*Filch*. Sir, Black Moll hath sent word her tryal comes on in the afternoon, and she hopes you will order matters so as to bring her off.
>
> '*Peachum*. Why, she may plead her belly at worst; to my knowledge she hath taken care of that security. But as the wench is very active and industrious, you may satisfy her that I'll soften the evidence … But 'tis now high time to look about me for a decent execution against next sessions. I hate a lazy rogue, by whom one get nothing 'till he is hanged. A register of the gang [*reading.*] … Tom Tipple, a guzzling, soaking sot, who is always too drunk to stand himself, or to make others stand. A cart is absolutely necessary for him.'[95]

In fact, it is from Wild's register of thieves that we get our term 'double cross'; when he was about to give one of them up to the authorities, he placed two crosses by their name.

In time, Wild's fortune amounted to approximately £10,000. He divided up the country into districts and appointed thieves to operate in each one, and he also had warehouses full of stolen goods on the continent. His sole motivation was the acquisition of profit. Yet the people thought that he was doing a good job, and even the government sought his recommendations in their attempt to stem what they perceived was an ever-rising level of crime. He was fast becoming a gentleman, dressing in fine lace and carrying a sword with him at all times. He was reaching the heights of respectability. After his death, the author of his biography berated the general public for having been duped by him:

> 'How infatuate were the people of this nation all this while! Did they consider, that at the very time that they treated this person with such a confidence, as if he had been appointed to the trade, he had, perhaps, the very goods in his keeping, waiting for the advertisement for the reward, and that perhaps, they had been stolen with that very intention?'[96]

Throughout his whole career, Wild never personally handled the goods himself. But slowly, public opinion began to turn against him, especially as a result of his vendetta against the young, fairly likeable rascal, Jack Sheppard. Wild was even attacked in court and stabbed in the neck by one of Sheppard's accomplices, Blueskin, in front of a judge.

After Sheppard's execution in November 1724, Wild's criminal empire began to crumble. The captain and the mate of a sloop which he used to ship stolen goods over to his warehouses on the continent had a quarrel because the captain had deducted the value of some missing lace from the mate's pay. The mate then decided to tell the revenue officers what had been going on. Wild's warehouses were searched, with Wild maintaining that all of the goods in them belonged to the captain, Johnson, who was then ordered to pay the tax man £700. Financially ruined, the captain decided to turn once again to his old profession of thieving to make ends meet, in partnership with another thief, Thomas Edwards, the landlord of a pub in Long Lane which had long been known to harbour thieves. One night, Johnson and Edwards began quarrelling, quite loudly, about the division of their booty, and they were both arrested by constables. Wild stood bail for

Johnson who was released forthwith, and Edwards was not charged with anything as there was no evidence against him. The latter was determined to get his revenge upon Johnson, and over the course of a few days diligently searched all of Johnson's known hangouts. Then one day, Edwards met Johnson in Whitechapel, and immediately called for a constable to have him arrested. When the constable laid hands upon Johnson he immediately demanded Wild's attendance. Wild attended with another of his trusted henchmen, a man named Quilt Arnold. It was not in Wild's interest that Johnson should be arrested, and so he urged Arnold to incite a riot among the locals. It is not known why the people in this district rioted, but, this being the era of King Mob, it was probably occasioned by some minor grievance in the district that had been building up over time – people even rioted over the price of gin in 1743. The tumult which followed provided Johnson with a perfect opportunity to escape from the law.

Someone, perhaps Edwards or the arresting constable, then informed the authorities of Wild's part in helping a prisoner to escape justice. Wild, therefore, decided to leave London and spend three weeks in the country, in the hope that the whole affair would just blow over. His return to London proved to be a big mistake, as the high constable of Holborn arrested Wild and Arnold at Wild's residence and hauled them before Sir John Fryer on the charge of aiding the escape of a prisoner. Both men were thrown into Newgate. On 15 February 1725, a list of charges was drawn up against Wild:

I.   That for many years he had been a confederate with great numbers of highwaymen, pickpockets, housebreakers, shop-lifters, and other thieves.

II.   That he had formed a kind of corporation of thieves, of which he was the head or director; and that notwithstanding his pretended services, in detecting and prosecuting offenders, he procured such only to be hanged as concealed their booty, or refused to share it with him.

III.   That he had divided the town and country into so many districts, and appointed distinct gangs for each, who regularly accounted with him for their robberies. That he had also a particular set to steal at churches in time of divine service: and likewise other moving detachments to attend at Court on birthdays, balls, &c, and at both houses of parliament, circuits, and country fairs.

IV. That the persons employed by him were for the most part felon convicts, who had returned from transportation before the time for which they were transported was expired; and that he made choice of them to be his agents, because they could not be legal evidences against him, and because he had it in his power to take from them what part of the stolen goods he thought fit, and otherwise use them ill, or hang them, as he pleased.

V. That he had from time to time supplied such convicted felons with money and clothes, and lodged them in his own house, the better to conceal them: particularly some against whom there are now informations for counterfeiting and diminishing broad pieces and guineas.

VI. That he had not only been a receiver of stolen goods, as well as of writings of all kinds, for near fifteen years past, but had frequently been a confederate, and robbed along with the above-mentioned convicted felons.

VII. That in order to carry on these vile practices, and to gain some credit with the ignorant multitude, he usually carried a short silver staff, as a badge of authority from the government, which he used to produce when he himself was concerned in robbing.

VIII. That he had, under his care and direction, several warehouses for receiving and concealing stolen goods; and also a ship for carrying off jewels, watches, and other valuable goods, to Holland, where he had a superannuated thief for his factor.

IX. That he kept in pay several artists to make alterations, and transform watches, seals, snuff-boxes, rings, and other valuable things, that they might not be known, several of which he used to present to such persons as he thought might be of service to him.

X. That he seldom or never helped the owners to the notes and papers they had lost unless he found them able exactly to specify and describe them, and then often insisted on more than half the value.

XI. And, lastly, it appears that he has often sold human blood, by procuring false evidence to swear persons into facts they were not guilty of; sometimes to prevent them from being

evidences against himself, and at other times for the sake of
the great reward given by the government.[97]

It was difficult for the prosecutors to make some of these charges stick. For
example, though the authorities had found warehouses full of stolen goods,
Wild disavowed any knowledge of these places and maintained that they
belonged to other people. Furthermore, much of the evidence against him
was based upon information received from disgruntled thieves formerly in
his employ. While any evidence is better than no evidence at all, it could be
reasoned that these were men would say anything in the hope of avoiding
the noose. What could bring down this master criminal?

Lace – that delicate fabric which adorned fine ladies' and gentlemen's
clothes – would be Wild's downfall. Lace was an expensive, prized
commodity during the eighteenth century. Laws were even enacted against
cut-price lace smuggled in from the continent, such was the value of it.
Between his return to London and his arrest and imprisonment, Wild
decided to assist a lady named Catherine Stretham to recover some lace
that had been stolen from her shop. She got most of it back, but was most
unimpressed with Wild's service, and suspected that he had in actual fact
been acting as a fence in this particular case. When the authorities became
aware of this, they simply decided to prosecute him under the old law
against receivers of stolen goods. The jury found him guilty and he was
sentenced to be hanged.

The man who had condemned so many criminals to death once they had
outlived their usefulness would meet the same end. During his final days
in prison, Wild proved to be an utter coward, in contrast to Jack Sheppard's
unfazed, almost heroic attitude towards his fate just six months earlier. Wild
petitioned the king in vain for a reprieve. His appeal for mercy having been
met with a swift rebuff, he attempted to take his own life by overdosing on
laudanum. He probably did not take enough, as it only induced a state of
extreme drowsiness. Then, on 24 May 1725, Wild was placed into the cart
and made his procession through London to Tyburn. While the public in
attendance had often treated petty thieves and highwaymen with a degree
of sympathy on their journey to be hanged, they were vitriolic in their
condemnation of Wild. As he passed in the cart he was pelted with dirt and
stones. He was hanged and buried in the Old Church at St. Pancras.

Wild was by no means the only agent of law enforcement to bear
a negative reputation. Alexander Smith, the author of the *History of the
Highwaymen*, wrote *The Comical and Tragical History of the Lives and*

Adventures of the Most Notorious Bayliffs in 1723. In the latter, Smith highlights the often dubious double lives bailiffs and constables led, with many of them being, or having been, highwaymen. Jack Hicks was one such fellow who, finding the life of a robber too tiresome, decided instead to become a gaol-keeper and then a constable. As a man of low morals, however, he died in a public house near Newgate gaol, 'a martyr to love, for an inveterate pox translated him out of this world into another'.[98] Another officer named William Browne – Smith thought that was his name anyway, although he says it could have been Leonard, but Smith was probably unconcerned with getting the details right anyhow – was both a bailiff and had a secret occupation as a counterfeiter of money.[99]

Wild was the most notorious of these officials-turned-rogues, however, and featured in many literary works during the eighteenth and nineteenth centuries. The lengthiest treatment of his life was Fielding's *The History of the Life of Mr. Jonathan Wild the Great* (1743). It is a fusion of satire and criminal biography. At the outset, Fielding explains himself to the reader, telling them why he has decided to designate this reprehensible man 'the Great'. All the great men of history, Fielding says, are in effect bad people:

> 'Greatness consists of bringing all manner of mischief on mankind, and Goodness in removing it ... In the histories of Alexander and Caesar, we are frequently, and indeed impertinently, reminded of their benevolence and generosity, of their clemency and kindness. When the former had with fire and sword overrun a vast empire, had destroyed the lives of an immense number of innocent wretches, had scattered ruin and desolation like a whirlwind, – we are told, as an example of his clemency, that he did not cut the throat of an old woman, and ravish her daughters, but was content with only undoing them.'[100]

In a further snipe at Julius Caesar, and in order to show just how skewed humanity's ideas of greatness can be, Fielding further argues that,

> 'When the mighty Caesar, with wonderful greatness of mind, had destroyed the liberties of his country, and with all the means of fraud and force had placed himself at the head of his equals, had corrupted and enslaved the greatest people whom the sun ever saw; we are reminded, as an evidence of his generosity, of his largesses [gifts] to his followers and tools, by

whose means he had accomplished his purpose and by whose assistance he was to establish it.'[101]

Fielding beguiles his readers into thinking that Wild is a hero, and proceeds to write about his 'hero' as though he were some illustrious person, exercising all the qualities of 'great' men. For example, when he works behind the scenes to have one of his own friends imprisoned in Newgate, Wild immediately goes to visit his friend in gaol, 'for he was none of those half-breed fellows who are ashamed to see their friends when they have plundered and betrayed them.'[102] Furthermore, the great man Wild has nothing but contempt for good men. This is shown by his treatment of an old school friend called Mr. Heartfree. Fielding writes that this Mr. Heartfree:

> 'Had several great weaknesses of mind; being too good-natured, friendly, and generous to a great excess. He had, indeed, little regard for common justice ... his life was extremely temperate, his expenses solely being confined to the cheerful entertainment of his friends at home.'[103]

Of course, the reader secretly wants to sympathise with Heartfree, especially when Wild moves to have him committed to gaol and hanged. Towards the end of the novel, however, Fielding tells the reader that they were silly all along to admire such a creature as Wild. When he is finally arrested for being a receiver of stolen goods, Fielding lists the qualities of this 'great' man in great detail, so that his readers too would know when they came across 'greatness' in a fellow and avoid them. Fielding's Jonathan Wild then sets out his maxims for being a great man, of which a few are set out below:

1. Never to do more mischief to another than was necessary to the effecting his purpose; for that mischief was too precious a thing to be thrown away.
2. To know no distinction of men from affection; but to sacrifice all with equal readiness to his interest.
3. Never to communicate more of an affair to the person who was to execute it.
4. Not to trust him who hath deceived you, nor who knows that he hath been deceived by you.
5. To forgive no enemy; but to be cautious and often dilatory in revenge.

6. To shun poverty and distress, and to ally himself as close as possible to power and riches.
7. To maintain a constant gravity in his countenance and behaviour, and to affect wisdom on all occasions.
8. To foment eternal jealousies in his gang, one of another.'[104]

Critics have interpreted Fielding's *Jonathan Wild* as a satire upon the Whig Prime Minister, Sir Robert Walpole (1676–1745). Walpole was the first Prime Minister of the Kingdom of Great Britain, and, in Fielding's view, entrenched his power in the world of courtiers and MPs in the same way that Wild set himself up as the master of London's low-life and thieves. Walpole was regularly lampooned in the press, and even was equated with Robin Hood on occasion. Indeed, Walpole was known as 'the Great Man' in England during the eighteenth century. It should be noted, however, that Fielding often distanced himself from any accusation that his novel was a satire upon Wild; Walpole ordered ten sets of Fielding's *Miscellanies* on royal paper at a cost of twenty guineas, and it would have been ungrateful of Fielding thereafter to claim *Jonathan Wild* as a satire upon his generous patron.

Wild's literary afterlife lasted into the nineteenth century, and he is usually the villain in the Jack Sheppard penny dreadfuls. Wild is also the villain in *Where's Jack?* (1969). When his tale is told as part of a Sheppard story, although both he and Wild are criminals, it is Wild who emerges as the confirmed baddie. Although stories of Jack Sheppard went out of fashion in the Edwardian period, Wild's 'afterlife' lived on. Because he was the epitome of the enterprising and intelligent master criminal, Wild inspired Arthur Conan Doyle's Professor Moriarty, the arch-nemesis of Sherlock Holmes, who first appeared in *The Final Problem* (1893). Until recently, people could get face to face with the real Jonathan Wild, for his skeleton was housed in the Hunterian Museum in London.

Chapter 10

Dick Turpin: The Knight of the Road

It was then, for the first time, that the thoughts of executing his extraordinary ride to York flashed across him...his pursuers were now within a hundred yards, and shouted him to stand...the whole of the neighbourhood was alarmed by the cries, and the tramp of horses...suddenly three horsemen appear in the road; they hear the uproar and din. "A highwayman! A highwayman!" cry the voices: "Stop him! Stop him!" But it is no such easy matter. With a pistol in each hand, and his bridle in his teeth, Turpin passed boldly on. His fierce looks – his furious steed – the impetus with which he pressed forward bore down all around him.

William Harrison Ainsworth,
Rookwood (1834)

If you were to ask an English person if they could name a famous historical thief, they would usually point to Robin Hood. Alternatively, they might also name Dick Turpin (1705-39), a famous highwayman who was, according to contemporary accounts, 'not only the terror but the talk of [the] country.'[105] After his death, Turpin's story was taken up by novelists such as William Harrison Ainsworth (1805-1882) and later by children's authors, and in the twentieth century by screenwriters. And his story was parodied in the movie *Carry on Dick*, in which the title character, Big Dick, shows off his 'huge weapon', and finally by Adam Ant in his song *Stand and Deliver!* Turpin is generally thought of as a good-looking, gentlemanly ladies' man, but as we will see, the reality was somewhat different; he was a thug who did not hesitate to use violence against his victims.

A pamphlet entitled *The Genuine History of the Life of Richard Turpin, the Noted Highwayman* (1739) provides the majority of information that we know of the eponymous highwayman's life. Turpin was born in East Ham, Essex. From an early age he was given a good education, being taught to read and write under the supervision of a tutor, Mr. Smith. His writing skills, as we will see, would later be the cause of his downfall. Having completed his rudimentary studies in reading and writing, he was apprenticed to a butcher in Whitechapel, London. Unlike some of the other highwaymen who have featured in this book, however, Turpin did not eschew this employment but successfully completed his apprenticeship, after which he returned to East Ham and set up his own business. While there, he married the daughter of a Mr. Palmer who resided in the area. However, in economic terms, entering the meat trade could be a risky business. The once proud butchers' trade, a profession which had boasted its own guild during the medieval period, faced competition from the emerging free market in meat. No longer did the Worshipful Company of Butchers (est. 1375) act as the gatekeepers to the trade. As a result, the market was saturated with unregulated tradesman, and many butchers had to make ends meet through often dubious means. To recoup some of his expenses, Turpin took to stealing his neighbours' livestock, cutting them up, and selling them in his shop. He carried on his business in this manner and evaded detection for some time. However, it was not to last; one evening he stole two oxen from a local gentleman named Mr. Plaistow. As Turpin was leading the animals back to his house, he was seen by two of Plaistow's servants. The two men followed Turpin and watched through the window as he cut up the animals, so they promptly returned home to tell their master.

A warrant was drawn up by the local Justice of the Peace and constables were sent to Turpin's house to arrest him. He saw them from an upstairs window and made preparations for his escape. His wife gave him a small amount of money and he escaped through a window at the rear. Knowing that his reputation in the county was utterly shot to pieces, he decided to commence a career as a smuggler. His tenure as a smuggler did not last long, however, because he soon became acquainted with a gang of deer stealers who went by the name of the Gregory Gang who operated around Essex Forest, whose members were Gregory, Rose, Fielder, and Wheeler. Deer stealing was rife during the eighteenth century; two particularly notorious gangs of poachers, who both earned the nickname of the Waltham Blacks because they used to blacken their faces when carrying out their raids, operated around Hampshire and Essex in the early eighteenth century, and their infamy even earned themselves a place in Daniel Defoe's *A Tour Through the Whole Island of Great Britain* (1724). The early eighteenth century was a time when common lands, which had previously been available for poorer people to farm on and use, were purchased by wealthier landowners and enclosed. In combination with already onerous game laws, there was a lot of resentment from members of society's poorer ranks towards the landowners, and, out of sense of social injustice, the Waltham Blacks decided to do something about it. The first notorious case occurred in October 1721 when they stole a number of deer from the Bishop of Winchester's lands in Farnham. Soon their targets got bigger, on one occasion stealing a large shipment of the king's wine. Their actions led to the passage of the Black Act in 1723. It stipulated that the death sentence could be used for any person found bearing arms in a royal forest, chase, or down. Thus, Turpin and the Essex gang were playing a dangerous game, for poaching was often punished to the full extent of the law.

Under Turpin's direction, the gang began to diversify their activities, and they started robbing country houses. The first such robbery was committed from the house of a chandler, Strype. The gang's real thug-like nature is revealed, however, in an account of their robbery from an old woman's house at Loughton, on the borders of Epping Forest, and who they believed was in possession of £700. The gang forced their way into the woman's house and blindfolded her and her maid. They demanded to know where the woman was keeping her money, but she refused to tell them. So they decided to make her sit on the fire, and the gang kept her writhing in agony until at last she told them where the money was. In total, they got away with £400.

With such a sum to divide between only four people, one would think that it would be enough for them to leave a life of crime behind and lead a respectable way of life. But there were rich pickings to be had from the houses of wealthy families in this part of the country. From a farmer in Essex the gang got another £700, although Turpin soon squandered his share because he enjoyed living the good life in the capital. Further robberies were committed, and some were more violent than that committed upon the old woman. Their most notorious robbery was committed upon the house of a Mr. Lawrence who lived in Edgware. Forcing their way into Lawrence's house, the ruffians gathered all the men into the same room and demanded to know where his money was. Lawrence did not have much money in the house at the time, and the best they could do was to ransack the upstairs and take off with some silver plate.

While even the short account of Turpin and his gang's escapades given thus far should in theory be enough to dispel any idea that the famous robber was a polite and courteous gentleman, the following crime committed at Lawrence's house will likely lower him further in readers' estimations.

Turpin was conducting a search of the upper rooms with Lawrence, another member of the gang was searching the lower part of the house. In the buttery, he found the maid cowering in the dark, most likely scared out of her wits. The man raped her. Contemporary biographies relate this in a very matter-of-fact way, and in some cases downplay it. The main source on Turpin's life, for example, simply says that the man 'debauch'd the servant maid'.[106] Smith does list several highwaymen in his compendium who were also 'ravishers', though he does not, like the Turpin biography, enter into significant detail of those occurrences. Rape was punishable by death in the eighteenth century but it was difficult to prosecute, even more so than it is nowadays. Idealists such as William Blackstone, the author of *Commentaries upon the Laws of England* (1765–69), argued that English law was enlightened because it held that in certain circumstances even a prostitute could bring an accusation of sexual assault against a nobleman and that she would be believed. This was in contrast to laws in France and elsewhere where it was, Blackstone assumed, near impossible for the same type of case to be brought. Of course, Blackstone's views were idealistic, for in rape cases much of the evidence brought by the victim depended upon her credibility. When a prostitute named Elizabeth Galloway brought a prosecution against Lord Drummond in 1715, Galloway was confined in Newgate for five days before the case was dismissed without progressing further. Recognising how difficult it was to obtain a conviction, Sir Richard Steele in *The Tatler* (1709–10) said that in rape cases it made no sense to have juries composed entirely of men. Juries in these instances should instead contain an equal number of men and women.[107] This quite modest and reasonable proposal of Steele's was never adopted by the authorities.

The news of the rape of the maid and the robbery at Lawrence's house became so notorious that the king issued a proclamation advertising a reward of 50 guineas and a promise of immunity from prosecution to any member of the gang who was willing to turn evidence against his accomplices. For the moment, however, no member of the gang seemed willing to betray his associates and they went on to commit another notorious robbery on the house of Francis, a farmer who lived in Marylebone. The women of the house, Francis's wife, daughter, and maid, were all cruelly beaten, and the robbers took off with a considerable but unspecified amount of money, along with several gold rings and a gold watch.

The reward for the gang's apprehension was now increased to £100, and Thompson, the keeper of Newgate, decided that he would try to track them down. Thompson learnt one night that the gang were all enjoying themselves in a tavern in Westminster. Thompson and his men burst through the door and managed to arrest three of them; Fielder, Rose, and Wheeler. However, Turpin escaped out of a window and rode away from his would-be captors. As a result of Wheeler having turned King's Evidence against Fielder and Rose, he was spared the hangman's noose.

Turpin's narrow escape from the law did not induce him to leave his criminal life behind, however, for he decided to become a highwayman. While travelling to Cambridge he came across a well-dressed gentleman. With his pistol at the ready, Turpin approached the man and commanded him to hand over all of his money. The man simply laughed at Turpin, for the man he had stopped was the gentleman highwayman, Tom King, who said to him; 'What! Dog eat dog? – Come, come, brother Turpin, if you don't know me, I know you, and should be glad of your company.'[108] Turpin had found himself a new partner in crime, and the pair swore loyalty to each other.

As both men's names were notorious throughout the surrounding area, and knowing that no landlord would take them in, the pair made a cave just off the King's Oak Road their hideaway. The cave was big enough for them to quarter their horses, and they were kept supplied with food and drink by Turpin's wife, who used to stay with him in the cave when King was absent. From here, they would ambush passengers who looked unlikely to put up any type of resistance. Turpin and King, having committed several notorious crimes together, the authorities began to actively hunt the pair down. It soon occurred to Turpin that Epping Forest would not be a safe haven for him. This was especially the case after he fatally shot the keeper of the forest. Bloodhounds were sent after him and unable to lose them solely by running away, he climbed a tree and waited for them to pass. It was while he was waiting in the tree that he resolved to leave the district entirely and go to a place where he was not known. He chose for his destination the county of Yorkshire.

Although some nineteenth-century stories of Turpin say that he heroically rode from London to York in one day upon his faithful horse, Black Bess, his earliest biographies record no such feat. While in Yorkshire, he attempted to set up in business as a horse-trader and, under the assumed name of John Palmer, became acquainted with and maintained cordial relationships with local traders and landlords. His residence in Yorkshire might have been the perfect chance for him to leave his criminal past behind and to begin anew, but he ruined things for himself one day. In October 1738, as he was returning from a shooting match, he saw one of his landlord's cocks in the street. He aimed his gun at it and killed it on the spot. An acquaintance of Turpin's, Mr. Hall, saw him do it, and warned him that, 'you have done wrong, Mr. Palmer, in shooting your landlord's cock'.[109] Turpin brushed off the remark, but Hall and the landlord subsequently went to the local justice of the peace and obtained a warrant for Palmer's arrest. At his examination, the judge asked Turpin if he could provide the names of any people who could testify to his good character. Being new to the area, and still under the assumed name of Palmer, he could not. Turpin was then questioned about his trade, to which he replied that he was a horse dealer, and conducted his business around Yorkshire and Lincolnshire. A man's character or standing in the local community counted for a lot in the eighteenth century criminal trial; lawyers did not generally appear for the accused, for it was reasoned that a person who was not guilty of crime did not need to 'prove' his defence. The likelihood of a person's guilt could thus be either proved or disproved according to how many people testified to the defendant's good character. Even when a person was convicted of a capital crime, their previous character could have a bearing upon whether they received the sentence of death or a lesser sentence. To the authorities in Turpin's case, however, something just did not add up; here was a man who could produce no character witnesses at all from his former life, and could only give a very sketchy account of his past. He was thus committed to the House of Correction at Beverley in Yorkshire, and the following is apparently a letter that was sent to the governor of the house explaining the circumstances of his committal:

'To the Master, or Keeper, of the House of Correction in Beverley,

Whereas it appears to us, upon the information of divers creditable persons, that John Palmer, of Walton in the East Riding of the County of York, is a very dangerous person, and we having required sureties for his good behaviour, until the next General Quarter Sessions of the Peace, in the County of York, which he the said John Palmer hath refused to find; there are therefore to command you, to receive into custody the body of the said John Palmer, and him safely keep, until he shall be discharged by course of law; and hereof fail not at your peril.

'Given under our hands and seals the third day of October, 1738.'[110]

Meantime, the justice, as a result of 'divers creditable persons' having approached him separately, began to suspect that Palmer was a highwayman. The day after Turpin had been committed to the House of Correction, the judge decided to visit him and get to the bottom of the matter, demanding of him information as to his profession and his previous abodes. Turpin responded that,

> 'About two years ago he had lived at Long-Sutton in Lincolnshire, and was by trade a butcher; that his father then lived at Long Sutton, and his sister kept his father's house there; but he having contracted a great many debts, for sheep that proved rotten, insomuch that he was not able to pay for them,, he was therefore obliged to abscond, and come and live in Yorkshire.'[111]

The justice's further inquiries with the authorities in Lincoln revealed that John Palmer had actually been accused of horse stealing while he was residing in Lincolnshire but that he escaped from the arresting officers. The authorities in Lincolnshire, however, could not answer for the spurious origin story that Turpin had provided to the Yorkshire magistrate.

As Turpin had not managed to provide any satisfactory answers as to his origin or trade, and the justice at York smelling a rat, he was subsequently imprisoned at York Castle for four months. This allowed the authorities to conduct further investigations into this seemingly enigmatic man who could provide no fixed place of birth, and give them an opportunity to try him for the horse theft that he committed at Lincoln. Prisoners in Georgian Britain had to pay for their upkeep, so Turpin decided to write to his brother-in-law, Mr. Rivernall, who lived in Essex. For whatever reason, Rivernall refused to pay the postage on the letter so it was kept at the post office at Saffron Walden. The postmaster there was Mr. Smith, Turpin's old writing tutor. Smith immediately told the local Justice of the Peace that this John Palmer was the notorious highwayman, Richard Turpin. This news was then swiftly communicated to the authorities in York.

Turpin was sentenced to death and hanged at Micklegate Bar in York, on 7 April 1739. He was brave in the face of death, as *The Trial of the Notorious Highwayman Richard Turpin* (1739) records:

> 'He was carried in a cart to the place of execution, on Saturday, April 7th, 1739, with John Stead, condemn'd also for horse

stealing; he behav'd himself with amazing assurance, and bow'd to the spectators as he pass'd: it was remarkable that as be mounted the ladder, his right leg trembled, on which he stamp'd it down with an air, and with undaunted courage look'd round about him; and after speaking near half an Hour to the topsman, threw himself off the ladder, and expired in about five minutes.'[112]

Contemporary accounts say that the local people took his body and buried it in St. George's Churchyard. A grave reputedly containing his remains can still be found within the city limits, although several doubts have been cast over the veracity of this, and the novelist William Harrison Ainsworth found no trace of his grave when researching a novel in the 1830s.

The last robbery by a highwayman took place in 1831; industrialisation and urbanisation around the capital and in other major cities meant that would-be highwaymen had fewer places to hide; people were also carrying fewer coins about their persons, and favoured traceable banknotes; improved road travel and the extension of the turnpike system, in addition to the professionalization of the police, meant that towns and roads were more policed than they had been previously. All of these factors contributed to the decline of the 'profession' of highway robbery, and it certainly would not have lasted as a viable option for would-be criminals once railways had arrived in Britain. The end result of these factors was to diminish the fearsomeness of the figure of the highwayman and make him an object of nostalgia.

The fact that they were no longer feared meant that Victorian authors could fictionalise their lives and transform certain highwaymen into good-looking, gentlemanly figures, capable of heroic feats. This is what William Harrison Ainsworth does in *Rookwood: A Romance* (1834). The novel draws upon gothic influences, opening in a spooky churchyard with the sexton and the main protagonist, the allegedly illegitimate Luke Rookwood, discussing an old family curse. The other son and hitherto legitimate heir is Ranulph Rookwood. In typical gothic manner, in which long lost secrets are revealed, it is turns out that Luke is actually legitimate by way of a clandestine first marriage of Sir Piers and a Catholic woman, and that he stands to inherit the Rookwood estate. The novel becomes a battle between the two brothers and their respective families over who gets to inherit the estate. Moving the plot forward is a jovial character, a friend of Luke's, who goes by the name of Jack Palmer. The latter is of course a pseudonym for Turpin, who is truly a heroic, handsome, polite and chivalrous.[113] Ainsworth's *Rookwood*, along with Edward Bulwer Lytton's *Paul Clifford* (1830), revived the reputation of highwaymen despite the fact that these criminals' reputations had declined in the latter part of the eighteenth century. The reason for this is partially due to the fact that Ainsworth does not portray Turpin committing any criminal act. Instead, it is the aristocratic Rookwoods who are the real criminals because they 'continue their murderous ways' until they each fall victim to their own schemes.

One of the most famous scenes from the novel, and one which quickly entered into legend, was the time that Turpin rode from London to York in one day on his faithful steed, Black Bess, which of course is pure fiction, and the same feat was attributed by Daniel Defoe to a seventeenth-century highwayman named William Nevison, nicknamed 'Swiftnick'. Black Bess in *Rookwood* is a character in her own right. She is loyal to Turpin, and often warns him of danger. There is a tragic scene in the novel when she dies in sight of York Minster, having undertaken the famous epic ride there with her master:

> 'Another mile is past. York is near. "Hurrah!" shouted Dick; but his voice was hushed. Bess tottered – fell. There was a dreadful gasp – a parting moan – a snort; her eyes gazed upon her master, with a dying glare; then drew glassy, rayless, fixed. A shiver ran through her frame. Her heart had burst [… Turpin] stood weeping and swearing, like one beside himself. "And art thou gone, Bess!" cried he, in a voice of agony, lifting up his courser's head, and kissing her lips.'[114]

The reader does not witness Turpin's death in the novel, for he mysteriously disappears. Ainsworth only relates the manner of his demise, and concludes by calling Turpin the *great* highwayman or, 'the *ultimus Romanorum*, the last of a race, which (we were almost about to say, we regret) is now altogether extinct [...] with him expired the chivalrous spirit which animated successively the bosoms of so many knights of the road'.[115] Thus, we see him depicted as the heir of several great robbers in a ballad which Turpin sings:

> Of every rascal of every kind,
> The most notorious to my mind,
> Was the cavalier captain, gay Jemmy Hind!
> *Which nobody can deny.*

But the pleasantest coxcomb among them all,
For lute, coranto, and madrigal,
Was the galliard Frenchman, Claude Du-Val!
  Which nobody can deny.

[…]

A blither fellow on broad highway,
Did never with oath bid traveller stay,
Than devil-may-care Will Holloway!
  Which nobody can deny.

And in roguery nought could exceed the tricks
Of Gettings and Grey, and the five or six,
Who trod in the steps of bold Neddy Wicks!
  Which nobody can deny.

Nor could any so handily break a lock,
As Sheppard, who stood on Newgate dock,
And nicknamed the gaolers around him "his flock!"
  Which nobody can deny.

Nor did highwayman ever before possess
For ease, for security, danger, distress,
Such a mare as Dick Turpin's Black Bess, Black Bess!
  Which nobody can deny.[116]

Ainsworth's novel went on to inspire further portrayals of Turpin in popular culture, and he pops up in some unlikely places. Sergeant Troy in Thomas Hardy's *Far From the Madding Crowd* (1874) plays Turpin in a circus performance of *Dick Turpin's Ride to York*. In 1840, an anonymous broadside ballad entitled *Turpin's Ride to York* was published:

"Dick Turpin! Bold Dick! Hie away!" was the cry
Of my pal (who were startled, you'll guess.)
For the pistols were levell'd as bullets whizzed by
As I leaped on the back of Black Bess.
Three officers mounted, led forward the chase,
Resolved in the capture to share;

But I smiled at their efforts, though swift was their pace,
As I urged on my bonnie black mare.
  But when I've a bumper, what can I do less,
  Than the mem'ry drink of my bonnie Black Bess?

Hark away, hark away! Still onward they press,
As he say by the glimmer of morn;
Through many a mile on the back of Black Bess,
That night he was gallantly borne.
High over, my pet, the fatigue I must share,
Well clear'd, never falter for breath;
Hark forward, my girl, my bonnie black mare,
We speed it for life or for death.
  Yet when I've a bumper, what can I do less,
  Than the mem'ry drink of my bonnie Black Bess?

The spires of York now burst into our view,
But the chimes they were ringing her knell;
Halt, halt, my brave mare, they no longer pursue,
She halted, she staggered, she fell.
Her breathing was o'er – all was hushed as the grave,
Alas, poor Black Bess, once my pride,
Her heart she had burst, her rider to save,
For Dick Turpin she lived and she died.
  Yet when I've a bumper, what can I do less,
  Than the mem'ry drink of my bonnie Black Bess?[117]

This song, as well as other nineteenth-century songs about Turpin such as *Turpin Hero* (c. 1840), has been covered by numerous folk singers down to our own day, with the latter having been covered most recently by the appropriately York-based folk rock band Blackbeard's Tea Party. Henry Downes Miles wrote *Dick Turpin, the Highwaymen* (1839) which sold well and went through four editions. The penny dreadful publisher, Edward Harrison, published the long-running and highly successful saga *Black Bess* during the 1860s. In the latter story, Turpin teams up with a number of famous thieves from the eighteenth century, including the afore-mentioned Jack Sheppard (1702–24). During the twentieth century, a whole range of magazines entitled the *Dick Turpin Library*, published by Aldine, were printed for children. Very few novels were published during the twentieth century, but Turpin does appear in some films and television shows. Sid James portrayed Turpin, or, 'Big Dick', in *Carry on Dick* (1974). In typical 'carry on' style, Dick is a womaniser whose robberies are punctuated by several sexual escapades. Between 1979 and 1982, a television show entitled Dick Turpin was broadcast starring Richard O'Sullivan in the title role. Thus, while the historical Turpin was in reality an ugly thug, later authors and film-makers have transformed him into the epitome of the gentlemanly highwayman. Other notorious highwaymen appeared after Turpin. James Maclaine, the so-called 'gentleman highwayman' was one of them. There was also Jack Rann, or 'Sixteen-String Jack'. However, neither of these men went on to achieve 'immortal' fame in literature and film. It is Turpin who people remember most. Ainsworth's reinvention of Turpin was so influential that nowadays, when anyone thinks of eighteenth century highwaymen, they usually think of Turpin.

Chapter 11

Dr William Dodd: The Rogue Clergyman

My friends are gone! Harsh on its sullen hinge
Grates the dread door; the massy bolts respond
Tremendous to the surly keeper's touch
The dire keys clang, with movement dull and slow,
While their behest the ponderous locks perform:
And fastened firm, the object of their care
Is left to solitude, —to sorrow left.

William Dodd,
Thoughts in Prison (1777)

There is no doubt that the eighteenth-century criminal code, at first glance, was brutal in its treatment of the poor. It is frequently pointed out by many historians that during the Georgian period almost 200 offences became capital felonies. This observation led the neo-Marxist historians, E.P. Thompson, Douglas Hay, Peter Linebaugh, Cal Winslow, and John G. Rule in *Albion's Fatal Tree* (1975) to argue that the eighteenth-century 'Bloody Code', which is what the body of capital statutes is frequently called by historians, amounted to a reign of terror by the elite against the poorer classes. Some of the conclusions in *Albion's Fatal Tree* certainly had their critics, notably J.H. Langbein. In an article for *Past and Present* in 1983, Langbein argues that most of the victims who decided to prosecute crime were drawn from the petty bourgeois and the poor rather than the elite. Historians writing during the 1980s further tested these assertions to see if they stand up to scrutiny; it happened that there were many exceptions; when the offences were serious enough, criminals from the bourgeoisie and aristocracy could be punished with just as much ferocity as those from lower down the social scale. This was especially the case with the crime of forgery; it was classed, since at least 1351, as a form of High Treason because it entailed rebellion against the power of the state. During the eighteenth century, forgery was one of the most serious crimes that a person could commit. Georgian Britain was a polite and commercial nation; the rising bourgeoisie fuelled the growth of trade across the expanding British Empire which, at this period in its formation, was largely driven by private trading companies such as the East India Company, Hudson Bay Company, and the Royal African Company. Consequently, it was assumed by criminal biographers that nothing could be more harmful to the credit and commerce of a proud trading nation than that of the forging of notes.[118]

It is to the case of a notorious forger that we now turn; William Dodd was born in Bourne, Lincolnshire, on 29 May 1729. He was the son of a clergyman, also called William. Dodd was academically talented, and in 1754 he was enrolled at Cambridge University where he completed his Bachelor of Arts degree. He was a high achiever but, as all university students do, he also ensured he enjoyed himself while at university. In the words of a contemporary biography he became 'a zealous votary of the God of Dancing, to whose service he dedicated much of that time and attention which he could borrow from his more important avocations'.[119] His love of the good life eventually led him to quit his studies and move to the capital in order to become a professional author. In contemporary accounts such as *The Newgate Calendar* and even Dodd's account of himself, it is his move to London which marks the beginning of his descent into a life of sin:

> 'He entered largely into the gaieties of the town, was a constant
> frequenter of all places of public diversion, and followed every
> species of amusement with the most dangerous avidity.'[120]

In London, he met a woman named Mary Perkins whom he hastily married on 15 April 1751. Many of his friends judged this to be an unwise move because neither he nor she was very wealthy, and they were already acquainted with Dodd's predilection for partying. The couple subsequently moved into a house in Wardour Street, Soho. Upon learning of his hasty marriage, Dodd's father travelled down to London to visit him and try to talk some sense into him and tell him that now he was a married man he needed to make provisions for the future and get a stable job. It seemed to work for the time being and on 19 October of the same year he was ordained to the post of a deacon at Caius College, Cambridge. During this time, he devoted himself to his studies and even published a book entitled *The Beauties of Shakespeare* (1752). His efforts were finally rewarded when he was promoted to the post of curate under the Reverend Wyatt in West Ham where, according to contemporary accounts, he spent the happiest and most honourable moments of his life. Upon the occasion of Wyatt's death, Dodd succeeded him as vicar.

Things seemed to be going well for the once profligate youth. He even returned to education and completed his Master of Arts degree in 1759. He delivered several Lady Moyer's public lectures in St. Paul's Cathedral; funding for these lectures was bequeathed to the cathedral upon the death of the eponymous noblewoman, Lady Moyer, and they ran from 1719 to 1774. The lectures were designed to inform the public against the creeping Enlightenment thinking that applied principles of reason to faith. The great and the good were impressed with his talents; while studying for his MA he was employed by the Bishop of St. David's, who recommended him as a tutor for the Earl of Chesterfield's son. Private tuition was actually the preferred mode of education for the children of the aristocracy during the eighteenth century. He soon reached new heights in 1764 when he became chaplain to George III. In 1766, he even completed his Doctor of Laws degree at Cambridge University. However, things started to go wrong for Dodd in 1767 when he attempted to get the position to rector at West Ham. Disillusioned, he quit all of his lecturing appointments and moved back to London where he fell into his old profligate ways. He wanted to live like a gentleman and to this end he purchased a country house in Ealing. He squandered cash on buying expensive coaches, and he soon found that his income was insufficient to support his lavish lifestyle. A windfall came in the form of his winning £1,000 on the national lottery. The first English national lottery was set up by the Elizabeth I in 1569 and was used by the government to raise public funds. A second long-running lottery established by the government in 1694. With some of his winnings he bought shares in the building of Charlotte Chapel, Bloomsbury, and worked into the designs special pews for members of the royal family to attend, although they never did. In spite of his lottery win and his investments, he was soon in debt again. The salary that he earned from his new appointment to the living of Hockliffe, Bedfordshire, in 1772 was scarcely able to maintain him in his extravagant lifestyle. Subsequently, upon learning that the high-paying living of St. Georges in Hanover had recently become vacant due to the death of its incumbent, Dodd attempted to bribe his way into the position. He wrote an anonymous letter to the Lord Chancellor's wife, Lady Apsley, and offered her £3,000 if she could recommend Dodd for the post. The letter was soon traced to Dodd and he was dismissed from all existing posts.

He was mocked as a hypocrite in the press. As he was now *persona non grata* in polite society, he deemed it prudent to retire to continent. While he was in Geneva, he served as a private tutor, and when he went to France, as his autobiography records, 'he descended so low as to become the editor of a newspaper!'.[121]

Two years later, hoping that the furore around his attempted bribery had died down, he returned to England where he again took a post at Magdalen Chapel. And his congregation appeared to have forgiven him and the affair with Lady Apsley totally forgotten. Creditors, however, had not forgotten about him. Demands for money were pressing him almost daily. Under the name of his former pupil, Lord Chesterfield, he forged a bond for the amount of £4,200. Dodd's pretence would be that the young Lord Chesterfield was urgently in need of raising money, but that he wanted to do so anonymously which is why he entrusted his former teacher and friend with obtaining it. Dodd attempted to redeem the bond with several eminent businessmen who refused at first until Dodd's friend, a broker named Robertson, agreed to carry out the transaction. Robertson took the bond to two bankers, Fletcher and Peach, to pledge money against it. Everything seemed to be going as planned; Fletcher and Peach signed off on the bond and Dodd received in his hands a sum of over £4,000. Dodd had pretended that the money was for the young lord who desired complete discretion, and he probably did not count on the fact that the whole transaction would, in the end, have to be referred to Chesterfield for authorisation. When it came to the young nobleman's attention, he disavowed all knowledge of the transaction and his secretary, Mr. Manly, immediately obtained a warrant for the arrest of Fletcher, Peach, and Robertson. Dodd's role as the architect of the scam was quickly discovered. In view of the fact that it was Chesterfield's former tutor who committed the crime, Manly told Dodd simply to pay the money back, which Dodd immediately did.

Chesterfield may not have wanted to prosecute, but Robertson was furious, understandably, and gave evidence against Dodd to the Lord Mayor. Dodd was then charged with forgery. Dodd was aghast and could not understand why he was being charged at all. After all, had he not paid back all the money? Furthermore, he had been charged with forgery with intent to defraud, a capital crime, but he argued that the prosecution had not as yet proved his intent, although one would have thought that intent was implicit if in a person's actions if they actually forge a document. In front of the judge and the jury at the Old Bailey, Dodd made some very eloquent speeches highlighting how his sorry financial state had driven him to commit the forgery. The jury took less than ten minutes to decide that he was guilty on both counts but recommended mercy. The judge in this matter was less than impressed with the jury's recommendation of mercy. He had been legally convicted by a jury of his peers after all. Thus, at sentencing, the judge asked, 'Dr William Dodd, you stand convicted of forgery – what have you to say why this court should not give you judgement to die according to law?'[122] Dodd blessed the court with another one of his long-winded speeches which, at first glance, contained just the right amount of repentance which would hopefully see him shown mercy. Dodd even sank to the floor, seemingly overcome with 'mental agony'.[123] He probably hoped that this performance would make the judge inclined to show him mercy, but the judge, as reported in the *Newgate Calendar*, said,

'Doctor William Dodd, – You have been convicted of the offence of publishing a forged and countefeit bond, knowing it to be forged and counterfeited; and you have had the advantage which the laws of this country afford to every man in your situation, a fair, an impartial, and an attentive trial. The jury, to whose justice you appealed, have found you guilty; their verdict has undergone the consideration of the learned judges, and they found no ground to impeach the justice of that verdict; you yourself have admitted the justice of it; and now the very painful duty that the necessity of the law imposes upon the court, to pronounce the sentence of that law against you, remains only to be performed. You appear to entertain a very proper sense of the enormity of the offence which you have committed; you appear, too, in a state of contrition of mind, and I, doubt not, have duly reflected how far the dangerous tendency of the offence you have been guilty of is increased by the influence of example, in being committed by a person of your character, and of the sacred function of which you are a member. These sentiments seem to be yours; I would wish to cultivate such sentiments; but I would not wish to add to the anguish of your mind by dwelling upon your situation. Your application for mercy must be made elsewhere; it would be cruel in the court to flatter you; there is a power of dispensing mercy, where you may apply. Your own good sense, and the contrition you express, will induce you to lessen the influence of the example by publishing your hearty and sincere detestation of the offence of which you are convicted; and will show you that to attempt to palliate or extenuate it, would indeed add to the influence of a crime of this kind being committed by a person of your character and known abilities. I would therefore warn you against anything of that kind. Now, having said this, I am obliged to pronounce the sentence of the law, which is – That you, Doctor William Dodd, be carried from hence to the place from whence you came; that from thence you be carried to the place of execution, and that there you be hanged by the neck until you are dead.'[124]

In his own truly theatrical style, once he heard his sentence being read out he almost fainted, uttering the words 'Lord Jesus receive my soul!' He may well have been deserving of mercy, but this judge was not going to give it to him.

Dodd had many sympathisers among the middle and upper classes, notably the author, Samuel Johnson (1709-84), who organised a petition to the king for a pardon which collected over 37,000 signatures. Dodd personally wrote to many ministers of state asking for a pardon. Below is a copy of the letter he wrote the Prime Minister, Lord North (1732-92):

'11 June 1777
'My Lord,
I have committed a capital crime for which the sentence of the law has passed upon me; and whether that sentence shall be executed in its full rigour, may, perhaps, depend upon the suffrage of your Lordship. The shame and self-reproach with which I now solicit your commiseration, I hope no man will ever feel, who has not deserved to feel them like myself. But I will not despair of being heard with pity, when, under the terrors of a speedy and disgraceful death, I most humbly implore your Lordship's intercession. My life has not been wholly useless; I have laboured in my calling diligently and successfully; but success has inflamed my vanity, and my heart betrayed me. Violent passions have exposed me to violent temptations; but I am not the first whom temptation has overthrown. I have, in all my deviations, kept Right always in view, and have invariably resolved to return to it. Whether, in a prosperous state, I should have kept my resolution, public justice has not suffered me to know. My crime has indeed been atrocious, but

my punishment has not been light. From a height of reputation which perhaps raised envy in others, and certainly produced pride in myself, I have fallen to the lowest and grossest infamy; from an income which prudence might have made plentiful, I am reduced to live on those remains of charity which infamy has left me. When so much has been given to justice I humbly entreat that my life, such as it must now be, may be given mercy; and that your Lordship's influence may be employed in disposing our Sovereign to look with compassion on,
My Lord,
Your Lordship's Most Humble Servant,
William Dodd.'[125]

Still any hope of a reprieve was denied, something which caused Johnson much dismay, who stated 'surely the voice of the publick, when it calls so loudly, and calls only for mercy, ought to be heard'.[126] However, justice had to be *seen* to be equal. Unfortunately for Dodd, just over a year prior to the discovery of his forgery two brothers, Robert and Daniel Perreau, who were both of relatively humble status in life compared to Dodd, had been executed for forgery. This may have been the reason why the authorities in this matter were indifferent to Dodd's petitions for mercy.

While awaiting his execution, Dodd began writing *Thoughts in Prison* (1777). He also entertained a number of high-ranking guests and even provided religious instruction to his fellow prisoners. Then, on 27 June 1777, he was taken with two other prisoners to Tyburn. At the foot of the gallows he prayed with his two fellow prisoners, after which the noose was placed around his neck and he was hanged. In order to ensure that he would not suffer, the executioner himself pulled Dodd's swinging corpse down in order to snap his neck quickly. With the passage of the Forgery Act in 1861, forgery was downgraded in status from high treason to a felony, with a mandatory sentence of life-imprisonment.

Dodd was an awkward figure for many; here was a man who should not have been drawn into a life of crime. On the face of it, he was a respectable gentleman. His profession – that of a clergyman – should have meant that he should have stayed on the straight and narrow. While many of those who were hanged at Tyburn were from the poorer classes and were assumed to be 'born to be hanged', it was clear, especially in Dodd's case, that the middle and upper classes could often fall into a criminal course of life as much as their working-class counterparts could.

Conclusion

What more rogues still? I thought our happy times
Were freed from such, as from rebellious crimes.
But such will be: i' the best of times we find,
The worst of men: the law can't lawless bind.
It might be so, since nature thought it fit,
To give some naught but lands, to others wit,
But no estates, bestowing such a mind,
That can't within due limits be confin'd.
Hence depredations, thefts, nay worser facts,
Cheating and whoring, with unheard of acts:
For swimming for their lives, these misrules think,
'Tis better catch at anything, then sink.
Such was this rogue, esteem'd the worst of men;
Liv'd by his sword, his pregnant wit, and pen.
In short, pray pardon if I speak amiss,
I never read so arch a rogue as this.
Richard Head, *The English Rogue*
(London: H. Marsh, 1665)

The market for collections of short biographies of criminals' lives, such as those written by Alexander Smith and Captain Johnson, lasted into the nineteenth century. In 1774, we see the first *Newgate Calendar* published, which is essentially a collection of the texts of various 'last dying speeches' broadsides that had been popular since the sixteenth century. Further editions were published in five volumes by two lawyers, Andrew Knapp and William Baldwin, in 1824, and a two volume edition entitled *Chronicles of Crime; or, The New Newgate Calendar* appeared in 1841. Editions of Charles Johnson's *Highwaymen* book continued to be published in the early part of the century. The historian Charles Macfarlane wrote *The Lives and Exploits of Banditti and Robbers in all Parts of the World* (1833), which is intended as a serious discussion of banditry in Europe and the far-flung corners of the British Empire. He did have a sense of humour, however; in his preface he sardonically remarks that, 'were I a despot as potent as a Chinese Emperor, I would decree a destruction of all the ballads relating to brigandism, and would punish every teller of a story, or a tradition on that subject.'[127] Of course, Macfarlane had no qualms about publishing a lengthy two volume work which showcased the lives of rascals from all parts of the world.

Macfarlane's work is actually the most interesting book of highwaymen that was published at this time because he actually recorded interviews with some of the bandits he met while touring Italy. When traveling through the Abruzzi region during the 1820s, which was then part of the Kingdom of the Two Sicilies, he encountered a man called Passo di Lupo. This man was a former member of a fearsome gang of outlaws named the Vardarelli. This is the description of his appearance that Macfarlane gives: 'I was struck with the appearance of a fellow with the deep scar of an old wound across his swarthy brow, and his left arm in a sort of sling'.[128] Macfarlane's first question was to ask Lupo what motivated him to become a bandit, to which he replied that 'I was making love with a Paesana [a local village girl], and had the misfortune to give a blow of the knife to one I thought my rival.'[129] Understandably, the local authorities attempted to arrest Lupo for having killed a man, although Lupo himself viewed this as a wholly unreasonable persecution. In fairness to Lupo, however, the vendetta – the settling of feuds through violence – was a custom amongst both the elites and the plebeian classes between the Renaissance and the twentieth century, and it still persists among organised crime groups in Italy. Thus, Lupo's view of the authorities' apprehension of him as unreasonable should be viewed in context.

Lupo's brush with the law made him seek out the company of a famous group of brigands, the Vardarelli, who operated in Ponte di Bovino, a mountain range about thirty miles from his home in Monte Gargano. However, he was not welcomed with open arms at first. The brigands distrusted him at first, and he was effectively a prisoner in the camp for a number of weeks and not permitted to venture outside of it. Only after having proved himself to them by taking an oath administered by a local priest who ministered to the bandits was he finally allowed to accompany the robbers on their excursions. Nevertheless, Lupo looked back to his robbing days with nostalgia, as Macfarlane records that,

I thought the fellow's hawk-like eyes still beamed joyfully as he talked of stopping government mails and diligences,

and rich graziers from the fairs of Foggia; and as he told me,
how, at times, he had scoured the whole plain of Apulia and
crossed the mountains of Basilicata, and plunged into other
provinces – meeting nowhere a formidable resistance –
nearly everywhere an impunity of plunder.[130]

The band shared little brotherly love, however, as Lupo recalled that the
bandit chiefs kept the lesser people of the gang in a state of near poverty:
the *guappi*, or the bullies of the gang, kept the lion's share and threw
morsels only to those below them. Even when the minions did manage
to obtain some money, they could not go into the local town and live the
high life. Macfarlane says that Lupo recalled never being able to spend
the little money that he did get on the few luxuries he desired because the
townsfolk were generally hostile to them, which made it a no-go area. It
did not help the robbers' cause, of course, that they were indiscriminate in
whom they chose for their victims, for they robbed peasants as well as rich
farmers. The peasants were only left alone or given money if the outlaws
needed a hiding place in the winter months. Lodging in a peasant's house
then brought with it a further threat of being betrayed to the authorities
for the reward money. During the milder seasons, their accommodation
was scarcely more inviting as they slept in cold caves. As a result, food
could often be scarce, and Lupo recalls that often they were so hungry
that sheep were stolen from fields and eaten raw on the spot. Scarcity of
food meant that quarrels often broke out between the bandits. Duels were
conducted and these frequently resulted in the death of a gang member.
In his preface, Macfarlane states that 'the reader will not find my robbers
such romantic, generous characters as those that occasionally figure in
the fields of fiction. [You] will meet with men strangers to that virtuous
violence of robbing the rich to give to the poor'.[131] Through his interview
with Lupo, as well as the accounts that he gives of many of the other
brigands in his collection, he certainly fulfilled his aim, which was to
highlight the hardship and unromantic nature of a bandit's life.

However, what we see beginning in the 1830s is fictional accounts of
thieves beginning to dominate the market, and superseding the 'factual'
accounts of thieves as contained in *The Newgate Calendars*. This was
marked by the emergence of the so-called Newgate novel in 1830, named
after the notorious gaol in London, when Edward Bulwer Lytton published
Paul Clifford (1830), telling the story of the life of an eighteenth-century
highwayman. The same author followed up his success with another novel

entitled *Eugene Aram* (1832), which is an embellished account of the life of the eponymous murderer. It seemed as though the public wanted nothing else but Newgate novels. William Harrison Ainsworth went on to write *Rookwood* (1834), which transformed the highwayman Dick Turpin (1705-39) from a petty thug into a dashing, gentlemanly highwayman. Ainsworth next turned his attention to Jack Sheppard in his eponymous novel. As we have seen, his novel caused a great deal of controversy in the press, however, because a murderer in 1840 admitted at his trial that the idea for committing his crime came to him as a result of having read Ainsworth's novel. The days of historical highwaymen enjoying the limelight in the middle-class three-volume novel were over.

While historical criminals were, for a brief moment in the 1830s, popular subjects in fiction, real-life contemporary criminals lost their sympathetic support from the nineteenth-century general public. This is because the state grew increasingly stronger in this later period and so did its means of enforcing the law – notably through the establishment of the Metropolitan Police in London in 1829, with provincial police forces established in the following decades. While in the eighteenth century there had been resistance to the idea of a uniformed police force, by the nineteenth century, middle-class reformers had managed to convince many people of the necessity for a standardised system of law enforcement and prison reform. Such reforms included a move away from the mere prosecution of crime to the prevention of crime through increased policing activity and the long-term institutional management of offenders. Criminals who were about to die on the gallows, unsurprisingly, often earned the sympathy of Georgian spectators, but less sympathy was necessary for criminals who were not going to lose their lives but were being justly punished by being incarcerated.

Moreover, increasingly crime began to be reported in newspapers, and the victim became the central figure in these newspapers' often brief accounts and representations of crime. In contrast to criminal biographies, newspapers omitted lengthy explanations and justifications of why criminals had turned to a life of crime. This left many readers with the feeling that many criminals were often savage opportunists. For example, in 1798, *The Times* carried this very brief entry regarding one attack by a highwayman:

> The Post-Boy, carrying the Mail from Bromley to Sevenoaks last night, was stopped about 2 miles from Farnborough, between the hours of 10 and 11 o'clock, by a single highwayman, who

presented a horse-pistol and demanded the Mail, which the boy gave him. He offered the robber half a guinea, but he declined taking it.[132]

Newspapers were also broadly supportive of new policing and legal reforms which further contributed to their loss of public support.

Besides, there were new types of criminals for authors and journalists to focus upon, particularly those criminals who were connected with an urban underworld, and these found criminals were often represented in fiction in the a genre of literature termed the 'penny blood'. These were periodicals which were published weekly and sold, as their name suggests, for a penny, and were marketed towards adults from the working and lower middle classes. A staple of their output included supernatural gothic tales, as well as crime. And it is in 1844 that one penny dreadful – in my opinion the greatest work of crime fiction ever to have been written – was published; George William MacArthur Reynolds's *The Mysteries of London*, which was serialised between 1844 and 1848. Reynolds was inspired to write this after having read a French novel by Eugene Sue entitled *The Mysteries of Paris* (1842-43), which is a fictional portrayal of the Parisian criminal underworld. In Reynolds's novel, or what he termed was an encyclopaedia of tales, every type of vice and crime conceivable is portrayed. There is an aristocrat who lives with four prostitutes at his beck and call. We see white collar crime in Reynolds's novel; MPs, bankers, and members of the aristocracy conspire to defraud investors by setting up phony railway companies. A conman sets up his own church, proclaiming himself to be a messenger sent from God and declares that he must sleep with the youngest and prettiest maidens from his congregation in order to spread the 'seed' of the gospel. A loose and lascivious aristocratic lady seduces a goodly young vicar, after which he changes from being virtuous to being a completely degenerate, lustful, depraved, and libidinous cad. Low-life thugs from the criminal underworld not only rob and kill people of their own volition, but they are often employed by members of the criminal 'upperworld' to carry out foul deeds. A mother and her husband plot to take out their four-year-old daughter's eye because she will look like more of a charity case when she is begging on the street. Thus, Reynolds's novel is not simply a picture of crime in low life but gives a picture of crime in both high and low life, and shows the interactions between the two spheres of criminality. And the Victorian public loved this novel; although scarcely known to the general public today, it was actually one of the biggest-selling novels of the Victorian era, outselling Dickens'

Oliver Twist (1838). Reynolds then published a follow up to *The Mysteries of London* entitled *The Mysteries of the Court of London* (1848–56). The second serial was even longer than *Mysteries of London*, running into eight volumes of double-columned, minute typeface. Low life crime is featured in this serial, and in the novel, we see child prostitution rings, organised crime gangs, abductions, and robberies. Reynolds's chief intention with *The Mysteries of the Court of London*, as in *The Mysteries of London*, is to highlight the depravity of the aristocracy, who, it turns out, are just as criminal as their counterparts from the underworld.

Reynolds had had first-hand contact with some of the shady characters from the poorer areas of metropolis, particularly before he became successful as an author and publisher. Along with novels such as *Oliver Twist* by Charles Dickens, his novel shined a light upon the actions of the 'professional criminals' and the 'criminal classes' who lived in the metropolis. And we begin to see references to these types of criminals in popular culture and news reports, and even in official government reports. In the minutes of evidence for the Report of the Capital Punishment Commission (1865), for example, we find the commissioners speaking of 'The vast criminal class that holds sway in this country'.[133] The criminal class, it was assumed, were a class of people beneath the respectable working classes who, like professional criminals, existed solely upon the proceeds of crime. It was imagined that there were specific geographical locations that harboured members of this criminal class. The idea of a criminal class and of a criminal underworld was so convincing that it was, from the mid-Victorian period, appropriated by legislators and members of law enforcement. Along with Reynolds and Dickens, perhaps the person most responsible for giving impetus to the growth of this idea was Henry Mayhew who wrote a four volume social treatise entitled *London Labour and the London Poor* (1851). Mayhew travelled into some of the poorest districts of the capital and documented what he saw, often conducting interviews with paupers. Taking his cue from Henry Fielding, he divided the poor into three categories or groups: those that will work (the respectable working classes), those that can't work (the infirm, disabled, and the elderly), and those that won't work. It was in the last category that the criminal classes could be found, according to Mayhew.

Stories of medieval outlaws remained popular as a result of Scott's *Ivanhoe*, as we saw on the chapter on Robin Hood. Pierce Egan the Younger, one of Reynolds's lifelong friends. In his early years, Egan tended to focus on tales of medieval and early modern outlaws; *Robin Hood and Little John; or, The Merry Men of Sherwood* Forest was serialised between

1838 and 1840; *Wat Tyler; or, The Rebellion of 1381* appeared in 1842, as did *Adam Bell; or, The Archers of Englewood*. Egan's *Captain Macheath*, adapted from John Gay's highwayman musical *The Beggar's Opera* (1727), also appeared in the early 1840s, although it is notoriously difficult to date some penny bloods as, like Egan's *Captain Macheath*, their publishers often did not place the date of publication on the title page, and neither do any of the author's journals or diaries survive which might give a hint as to when they were working on certain ones. His novels were full of violence; the killing and maiming of soldiers of the law accompanied with scenes of attempted rapes and kidnappings. Both Egan, and especially Reynolds, came in for a lot of criticism in the press. For example, in 1861, *The Times* remarked that 'Lust was the Alpha and Murder the Omega' of both of these men's works.[134]

At the beginning of the 1860s, the sensation novel burst onto the scene. The genre was influenced by earlier gothic writing as well as the Newgate novel. Sensation fiction usually depicts tales of adultery, bigamy, theft, kidnapping, seduction, and murder in middle-class spheres of life. The first sensation novel is assumed to be Wilkie Collins's *The Woman in White* (1859-60), which involves cases of mistaken identity, presumed deaths, and white collar crime in the form of fraud and embezzlement. Other authors were quick to capitalise upon Collins's success; Charles Dickens' *Great Expectations* was serialised between 1860 and 1861; Ellen Wood wrote *East Lynne* (1861), and Mary Elizabeth Braddon wrote *Lady Audley's Secret* (1862). The themes of the genre were hardly new, as stories of vice and iniquity among members of the upper and middle classes had been around for a while. However, the genre was innovative in one respect; it paved the way for the foregrounding of the detective as the main protagonist in crime fiction. In tracing the 'first' detective novel, one encounters some quite heated academic debates. Various stories have been claimed as the original detective novel. Edgar Allen Poe's *Murders in the Rue Morgue* (1841) is often credited as one of the first American examples. Wilkie Collins's *The Moonstone* (1868) has also been credited as having started the genre. It should be noted however, that most Victorian novels have cases of false identity that must be exposed, hidden and sordid family secrets that are eventually revealed, or some fiendish plot that the protagonist has to expose. Whoever started the genre, it is clear that the genre reaches its high point with Conan Doyle's Sherlock Holmes stories, a private detective who first appeared in *A Study in Scarlet* (1887). Doyle presented middle-class Victorian readers with thrilling tales of crime in which the hero, Holmes, solved crimes in a 'scientific' manner, and the fictional detective anticipated several advances in police science before they were actually implemented by forces, notably the study of fingerprints.

However, while the heroes of middle-class crime fiction were by the latter half of the century those who pursued criminals, the highwayman and the street robber remained the hero in penny dreadfuls. These were cheap weekly magazines, similar to penny bloods, but targeted towards youngsters. Within their ranks were tales such as *The Wild Boys of London; or, The Children of the Night* (c.1866), which, because of its scenes of nudity and flagellation, was banned by the authorities.We can add to the wild boys' ranks stories such as the epic Dick Turpin saga *Black Bess; or, The Knight of the Road* (c.1866–68). The heroes of these tales were not all dead or fictional, for they often made heroes out of contemporary criminals; *Ned Kelly: The Ironclad Australian Bushranger* (1880) appeared while Kelly was still alive. Evidently, Kelly's fame travelled at lightning fast pace throughout the British Empire. These penny dreadfuls were blamed for the rise in juvenile crime by sanctimonious commentators in the Victorian press. Thus, with the backing of the middle-class press behind her, moralists such as Charlotte M. Yonge (1823–1901), to name but one example, sought to police the reading habits of young children:

> 'Wholesome and amusing literature has become almost a necessity among the appliances of parish work. The power of reading leads, in most cases, to the craving for books. If good not be provided, evil will only too easily be found [...] If the boy is not to betake himself to 'Jack Sheppard' literature, he must be beguiled by wholesome adventure. If the girl is not to study the 'penny dreadful,' her notions must be refined by the tale of high romance or pure pathos.'[135]

After forty years, the moral panic over Ainsworth's *Jack Sheppard* had still not died down, evident by Yonge's reference to it. Consequently, a whole range of tedious, snooze-inducing books appeared, all of which had moralist undertones, such as A.L.O.E.'s *The Robber's Cave: A Tale of Italy* (1882). Other examples include children's books written by Christian missionaries, such as A. Delver's *Below the Surface; or, Life in the Slums* (1885), which is a condescending portrayal of life among the so-called criminal classes of London's East End. This is not to say that penny dreadfuls featuring criminals as their heroes completely died out by the late 1800s, but it is clear that the direction of travel was favouring stories which either featured the detective as the protagonist or, in the case of children's books, usually featured middle-class philanthropists on a journey into the forgotten parts of London.

The works of Delver reflects the work being conducted by social workers and evangelicals at the time. Andrew Mearns authored *The Bitter Cry of Outcast London* in 1883, subtitled as 'An Inquiry into the Condition of the Abject Poor'. And some truly astonishing cases of immorality and criminality were found in Mearns's explorations into the poorer parts of London:

> Another apartment contains father, mother, and six children, two of whom are ill with scarlet fever. In another nine brothers and sisters, from 29 years of age downwards, live, eat and sleep together. Here is a mother who turns her children into the street in the early evening because she lets her room for immoral purposes until long after midnight, when the poor little wretches creep back again if they have not found some miserable shelter elsewhere. Where there are beds they are simply heaps of dirty rags, shavings or straw, but for the most part these miserable beings find rest only upon the filthy boards.[136]

The only thing which could ameliorate the depravity of the "lower classes" according to Mearns, being a clergyman, was, of course, religious instruction. In 1885 William T. Stead, a journalist for *The Pall Mall Gazette*, authored a series of articles entitled 'The Maiden Tribute of Modern Babylon' which purported to be 'the story of an actual pilgrimage into a real hell'. Stead showed readers how easy it was for somebody to purchase a child prostitute. Similarly, Charles Booth published *Life and Labour of the People in London*, which eventually ran to seventeen volumes, between 1889 and 1903, a publication which even contained a map of where the criminal classes could be found.

While this book was an attempt to revive the style of writing pioneered by Alexander Smith and Charles Johnson during the eighteenth century, in whose tomes the lives of the most notorious reprobates were chronicled and packaged up for an audience eager for excitement. For the most part, rogues, robbers, and scoundrels whose lives are depicted in this collection were drawn from society's poorer ranks. But it should be remembered that, while there has historically been a great deal of criminality amongst the poor, often their crimes are petty, and they pale in comparison to the crimes committed by upper class, or 'white collar' criminals such as the corrupt MP, the fraudulent banker, businessmen and their Ponzi schemes, the tax-evading corporation, to name but a few. As an author in *Fraser's Magazine* declared in 1834, 'the age of highwaymen has gone, that of cheats and swindlers has succeeded.' Yet rarely are the upper-class embezzlers caught, and they often get off comparatively lightly even when they are. For as the highwayman Captain Macheath in John Gay's *The Beggar's Opera* sings,

> But gold from law can take out the sting,
> And if rich men like us were to swing,
> T'would thin the land such numbers to swing,
> *Upon Tyburn Tree!*[137]

Appendix

Bulla Felix: The Roman Robin Hood

At this period one Bulla, an Italian, got together a robber
band of about six hundred men, and for two years continued
to plunder Italy under the very noses of the emperors and of
a multitude of soldiers. For though he was pursued by many
men, and though Severus eagerly followed his trail, he was
never really seen when seen, never found when found, never
caught when caught.

Cassius Dio

Although this collection of criminals' lives focuses principally upon English highwaymen, the account of Bulla Felix, the Roman Robin Hood, is included here in order to show that the 'profession' of banditry is an ancient one. As we will see, his story holds many similarities to that of the medieval Robin Hood. First, however, let us gain an overview of banditry in the ancient world. Pharaohs in Ancient Egypt enacted laws against the *apiru*, a word which roughly equates to our modern understanding of bandits. Sources from the Canaanites attest to the existence of groups of *habiru*. These were groups of armed robbers who sometimes acted as mercenaries. Even in the Bible we see reports of bandits. In the ninth chapter of Judges, we are told that 'the leaders of Shechem rebelled against Abimelech by putting bandits in the hills, who robbed everyone who travelled by on the road.'[138] Similarly, in the book of Ezra it is said that 'the hand of our God was on us, and he delivered us from our enemy and from bandits along the way.'[139] In the New Testament, Jesus uses a highway robbery to illustrate the story of the Good Samaritan.[140] When the Gospel of John tells us that Pontius Pilate releases a man named Barabbas from gaol instead of Jesus, at the behest of the crowd, the word used to describe Barabbas in Greek is *lestes*, meaning 'bandit'. And it was two brigands who were crucified with Jesus on the cross.[141] An apocryphal source, the Gospel of Nicodemus, reveals the names of the two brigands on the cross as Dimas and Gestas, with the latter being the unrepentant thief. (Although many English translations of the Greek scriptures simply state 'robbers' or 'criminals', the Greek word used means 'bandit'. Unsurprisingly, the names of many of these robbers and brigands from the ancient world have not survived. Perhaps the most famous bandit from antiquity, or the one whose name is known to posterity, at least, is the afore-mentioned Felix.

It is necessary, however, to briefly examine the state of law and order in Ancient Rome, and what conditions gave rise to banditry. The law code of Ancient Rome may have been sophisticated, but we do not know much about its systems of law enforcement. We know virtually nothing about policing in the days of the Roman Kings (753-509BC). In the days of the Roman Republic (509-27BC), we know that Rome had officials known as *aediles* who were responsible for the maintenance of law and order. As few free citizens were willing to serve as policemen, the *aediles* delegated the responsibility of policing largely to slaves. In the century leading up to Julius Caesar's dictatorship, this limited form of law enforcement was unable to deal with the riots and tumults which were characteristic of the political situation at this period. It was only during the reign of Augustus (6-14) that the Roman police force gradually assumed a semblance of organisation; a member of the Roman Senate was appointed as the city prefect; he was in charge of three army units known as the Urban Cohorts, which was in reality an extension of the Praetorian Guard. It is unclear if routine policing activities were undertaken by the Urban Cohorts, but they did maintain order at public festivals and gladiatorial games. An extension of the Cohorts was the Night Watch which kept order after dark. Those who had been caught committing a crime would be taken before a magistrate to answer the charge. Ancient Rome did not imprison its offenders, however, and prisons were merely places where felons were taken while they were awaiting trial and sentence.

In the provinces and outposts of the Roman Empire, it was the job of the governor to maintain order. All judicial power was vested in his hands. His authority ranged from overseeing relatively minor legal disputes over land and property and administering punishments to runaway slaves. Another task that the governor was charged with, according to *De Officio Praesidis* ('Concerning the Duties of a Governor), was the hunting down and punishment of bandits, or *latrones*, as the Romans called them. In order to carry out these duties, the governor had at his command the soldiers stationed in the provinces, and this could be quite a hefty force in some parts of the Roman world. For example, Strabo (d. 23AD), a Greek philosopher, tells us that the governor of Egypt had at his command 18,000 heavy infantry, 4,500 light infantry, and 1,500 cavalry ready to undertake policing duties. Thus, within his province, the governor held the same judicial power of emperor.

Yet even though both the capital and the provinces appear to have had a systematic approach to law enforcement, as systematic as the ancient world could be at any rate, essentially policing stopped at the city walls. It was dangerous for travellers to travel alone without any armed guards themselves, especially at times when the empire was in the midst of a civil war and competing emperors vied for power. When there is a great deal of political unrest in a country, the region becomes an ideal environment in which bandits can thrive.

Although Felix is the focus of this chapter, shortly before we find accounts of him in contemporary writings, we see reports of another bandit named Maternus, who flourished in Gaul, Spain, and Northern Italy around the year A.D. 183. The information about Maternus comes from the writings of Herodian, but Maternus is not an archetype of the noble robber who steals from the rich to give to the poor. His life and deeds are described in the following manner by Herodian:

> 'A former soldier named Maternus [...] had committed many frightful crimes. He deserted from the army, persuading others to flee with him, and soon collected a huge mob of desperadoes. At first they attacked and plundered villages and farms, but when Maternus had amassed a sizable sum of money, he gathered an even larger band of cutthroats by offering the prospect of generous booty and a fair share of the loot.'[142]

Maternus, not satisfied with being a mere bandit, conspired to depose the reigning Emperor Commodus (161–92). He was foiled in this attempt, however, for when he attempted to kill the emperor at a public festival he was seized and beheaded. Commodus was eventually assassinated and replaced by Pertinax (126–93). The reign of the latter was short-lived, and what followed in the year 193 was a period known as the year of the five emperors, with Septimius Severus (145–211) emerging victorious at its end.

In contrast to the brutish Maternus, Bulla Felix was a noble robber. He flourished in and around the hinterland of Rome between 205 and 207. Septimius Severus had deposed and ordered the execution of his predecessor, Didius Julianus in 193, and by 205 was engaged in warfare in Britain. Severus was a capable military leader, and was winning the war against the rebellious Britons, but he was annoyed that, in the public eye, he was viewed as no match for Felix.[143]

What little historians know of this Felix's life comes from the writings of Cassius Dio. As its title suggests, Dio's *Roman History* is an account of the history of Rome from its founding in 753BC right down to his own time, although only the parts covering the end of the Roman Republic and the early imperial period survive. There is some debate about precisely when *Roman History* was written, although most historians agree that the majority of it was completed in the 220s. Some of the details which Dio records in his history must naturally be taken with some scepticism. It is likely that Felix was indeed a historical figure, but whether some of the adventures ascribed to Felix in Dio's writings are true is open for debate. While he based a lot of his accounts upon facts, he was also prone to overdramatizing events as well. However, as we saw in earlier chapters, it was not uncommon for later crime writers to ascribe fantastical, often superhuman feats to their subjects.

We are told by Dio that Felix was an Italian who had at his command a force of six hundred men that 'for two years continued to plunder Italy under the very noses of the emperors and of a multitude of soldiers'.[144] We know little about his early life or why he became a bandit. He may have been born into a very poor labouring family, and in the days of the Roman Empire, and indeed further back to the days of Ancient Egypt, it was often humble shepherds who became bandits. They were often viewed as ne'er-do-wells, and had a reputation for being involved in petty crime. Alternatively, Felix may have been a soldier who had deserted from the army. Whole legions, if they found themselves on the losing side of one of Rome's many internal power conflicts, could effectively find themselves delegitimised and stuck in a foreign place without pay or provisions. The fact that Felix was able to command a formidable force of over six hundred men makes it more probable that he was a person with some military experience and not a lowly shepherd.

Whatever his social origins may have been, what is striking about the short account of Felix's life in Dio's writing is how much of his life and deeds resemble those of the medieval English hero, Robin Hood. For example, we are told that Felix upon occasion distributed some of his plundered wealth among the general population. While this has resonances with the idea that Robin Hood stole from the rich to give to the poor, it was of advantage to Felix to do this, for it made the local people loyal to him. Even when he robbed people upon the highway, Felix appears to have been a most agreeable robber. According to Dio's account, he only ever took a small portion of the money or goods that people had upon their person. If the traveller happened to be an artisan, he would detain them for a short time while he made use of their skills, and thereafter dismissed them with a gift of money or some other present in acknowledgement of services rendered.

Moreover, Felix was a master of disguise, as illustrated by the following episode; some of his men had been captured by the local magistrate (the precise details of where these events took place are unknown to us); the outlaws' sentence was to be fed to wild beasts as entertainment in one of the amphitheatres, a sentence known as *damnatio ad bestias* ('damnation to beasts'). He approached the centurion guarding his men and pretended to be the governor of a district. He told the soldier that he needed the men in question for some purpose, and to release the men forthwith, which the centurion did. At another time, he approached a centurion and said that if he followed him into the woods he would lead him to Felix. The centurion accompanied Felix to the forest, whereupon his men seized him. Then while the centurion was in Felix's custody, the latter decided to hold a mock tribunal by dressing up as a magistrate. The centurion's head was then shaved, and he was sent back to the authorities, having been ordered to tell them the following message: 'feed your slaves so that they may not turn to brigandage'. Such scenes mirror one of the occurrences in *A Gest of Robyn Hode* (c. 1450). Little John, under the assumed name of Raynolde Grenelefe, becomes a servant in the Sheriff's household. He convinces the Sheriff of Nottingham to enter the forest with him because he knows where Robin Hood can be found. The Sheriff eagerly assents to this, but once he is in the forest he is surrounded by Robin Hood and his men. Robin initially plans to keep the Sheriff as a hostage in the forest, but eventually he lets him go. Before Robin Hood allows the Sheriff to depart, he makes him swear an oath that he will never again attempt to harm Robin Hood or any of his men.

Felix had terrorised the Italian countryside for up to two years, and for Emperor Severus, enough was enough. From Britain, he sent a tribune along with a number of cavalry back to Rome to hunt down this notorious malefactor. And Severus threatened the tribune with a dire punishment should he fail to apprehend Felix.[145] It was clear to the tribune that the standard tried and tested tactics for arresting the brigand simply would not work. But how was he to capture him, and in the process, save his own skin as well? *De Officio Praesidis* goes on to state that, in the hunting down of bandits, governors 'must use force against their collaborators (*receptatores*) without whom the bandit (*latro*) is not able to remain hidden for long'.[146] Thus, the law recognised that, to successfully capture a bandit, a governor must work with those who are known to the bandit and convince them to betray him.[147] Like many of his bandit successors in the medieval and early modern periods, a woman would prove to be Felix's downfall. Fortuitously, the tribune learnt that Felix was having an affair with the wife of a Roman citizen. The tribune offered the husband and the wife immunity from prosecution if they would deliver up Felix to him to which they assented. He was given up, and subsequently captured while he was sleeping in a cave. Thereafter he was sentenced to *damnatio ad bestias* and his band was dispersed.

Even though we must treat Dio's account of Bulla Felix with a healthy degree of scepticism, it does appear to be one of the earliest instances we see of the figure of the noble robber in action. He treated the poor kindly, although perhaps it was more out of self-interest than any humanitarian motive. He was a master of disguise, and constantly eluded the authorities. Such was his popularity with his men and among the populace that, as with all good bandits, no decent member of society would ever betray him. Instead, people had to be bribed to give up Felix to the authorities. As we saw in previous accounts, betrayal was the means through which many later highwaymen would meet their deaths, for there was rarely true honour among thieves, and they were ever ready to betray one of their own to the authorities in return for leniency or a reward.

Further Reading

There are many historical and scholarly works which have assisted me in writing this book. References to them are given in the notes for each chapter. This bibliography, however, is intended to act as a guide for readers should they wish to learn more about highwaymen or eighteenth- and early nineteenth-century crime, or access some of the primary sources referred to in this book. Where there are no modern critical or popular reprints available, particularly in the case of novels and some of the works of Alexander Smith and Capt. Charles Johnson, I have given the web addresses where online versions of the texts may be found.

Ainsworth, William Harrison, *Victorian Bestsellers: Jack Sheppard: A Romance* (London: Penguin, 2010)

——, *Rookwood: A Romance* 3 Vols. (London: Bentley, 1839). Text available from the Internet Archive at https://archive.org/details/romancerookwood00ainsrich

Alexander, James W., 'Ranulf III of Chester: An Outlaw of Legend?' *Neuphilologische Mitteilungen*, 83: 2 (1982), pp. 152-157

Allingham, Philip V., 'The Victorian Sensation Novel, 1860-1880: "Preaching to the Nerves Instead of the Judgment"', in *The Victorian Web: Literature, History and Culture in the Age of Victoria*, ed. by George P. Landow, online edn. http://www.victorianweb.org

Alpert, Michael, Trans., *Lazarillo de Tormes and The Swindler: Two Spanish Picaresque Novels* (London: Penguin, 2003)

Baillie Reynolds, P. K., 'The Police in Ancient Rome', *The Police Journal: Theory, Practice and Principles*, 1: 3 (1928), pp. 432-42

Barnes, T. D., 'The Composition of Cassius Dio's "Roman History"', *Phoenix* 38: 3 (1984), pp. 240-255

Basdeo, Stephen, *The Life and Legend of a Rebel Leader: Wat Tyler* (Barnsley: Pen & Sword, 2018)

——, 'Robin Hood the Brute: The Outlaw in 18th-Century Criminal Biography', *Law, Crime and History*, 6: 2 (2016), pp. 54-70.

Carver, Stephen J., *The Life and Works of Lancashire Novelist William Harrison Ainsworth, 1805-1882* (Lampeter, NY: Edwin Mellen, 2003)

Defoe, Daniel, *A Tour Through the Whole Island of Great Britain* (London: Folio Society, 1970)

——, *Moll Flanders* (New York: Norton, 2004)

Dickens, Charles, *Bleak House*, ed. by Gill, Stephen (Oxford: Oxford University Press, 2008)

——, *Great Expectations*, ed. by Cardwell, Margaret (Oxford: Oxford University Press, 2008)

——, *Little Dorrit*, ed. by Keith Carabine (London: Wordsworth, 1996)

——, *Oliver Twist* (London: Penguin, 2012)

Dio, Cassius, *The Loeb Classical Library: Roman History* Trans. Cary, Earnest 9 Vols. (Cambridge, MA: Harvard University Press, 1927)

Dobson, R. B. & Taylor, J., eds., *Rymes of Robyn Hood: An Introduction to the English Outlaw* 3rd Edn. (Stroud: Sutton, 1997)

Doyle, Conan, *The Complete Works of Sherlock Holmes* (Bath: Parragon, 2015)

Emsley, Clive, *Crime and Society in England, 1750-1900*, 2nd Edn. (London: Longman, 1996)

Fielding, Henry, *Jonathan Wild*, ed. by Claude Rawson (Oxford: Oxford University Press, 2003)

Flanders, Judith, *The Invention of Murder* (London: Harper, 2011)

Fuhrrman, Christopher, *Policing the Roman Empire: Soldiers, Administration, and Public Order* (Oxford: Oxford University Press, 2011)

Gladfelder, Hal, *Criminality and Narrative in Eighteenth-Century England: Beyond the Law* (Baltimore: Johns Hopkins University Press, 2001)

Gay, John, *The Beggar's Opera*, ed. by Hal Gladfelder (Oxford: Oxford University Press, 2013)

Gray, Drew, *Crime, Policing and Punishment in England, 1660-1914* (London: Bloomsbury, 2016)

Grunewald, Thomas, *Bandits in the Roman Empire: Myth and Reality*, Trans. John Drinkwater (London: Routledge, 1999)

Hay, Douglas, Peter Linebaugh, John G. Rule, E. P. Thompson & Cal Winslow, *Albion's Fatal Tree: Crime and Society in Eighteenth-Century England*, rev. ed. (London: Verso, 2011)

Head, Richard, *The English Rogue described in the Life of Meriton Latroon*, ed. by Arthur Heyward (London: H. Marsh, 1665). Text available from *Early English Books Online* https://quod.lib.umich.edu/e/eebo/A43147.0001.001?view=toc

Herodian, *The History of the Roman Empire*, Trans. Echols, E. C. (Los Angeles: University of California Press, 1961)

Hitchcock, Tim, *Down and Out in Eighteenth-Century London* (London: Hambledon, 2004)

——, & Robert Shoemaker, *London Lives: Poverty, Crime, and the Making of a Modern City, 1690-1800* (Cambridge: Cambridge University Press, 2015)

Hobsbawm, Eric, *Bandits*, rev. ed. (London: Abacus, 2002)

Holmes, Ronald, *The Legend of Sawney Bean* (London: F. Muller, 1975)

Holt, James C., *Robin Hood* (London: Thames and Hudson, 1982)

Holmes, Richard, ed., *Defoe on Sheppard and Wild* (London: Harper Perennial, 2004)

Howson, Gerald, *Thief-taker General: the Rise and Fall of Jonathan Wild* (London: Hutchinson, 1970)

Johnson, Charles, *A General History of the Lives and Adventures of the Most Famous Highwaymen, Murderers, Street-robbers, &c.* (London, 1734; repr. London: O. Payne, 1736). Text available from the Internet Archive https://archive.org/stream/livesexploitsofe00whitrich

——, *Lives of the Most Remarkable Criminals*, ed. by Heyward, Arthur (London: Routledge, 1927)

——, *A General and True History of the Robberies and Murders of the Most Notorious Pyrates* ed. by Heyward, Arthur (London: Routledge, 1927)

Kaufman, Alexander, ed., *British Outlaws of Literature and History: Essays on Medieval and Early Modern Figures from Robin Hood to Twm Shon Catty* (Jefferson, NC: MacFarland, 2011)

Keen, Maurice, *The Outlaws of Medieval Legend* (London: Routledge, 1961)

Kinney, Arthur, ed., *Rogues, Vagabonds and Sturdy Beggars: A New Gallery of Tudor and Early Stuart Rogue Literature* (Amherst, MA: University of Massachusetts Press, 1990)

Knapp, Andrew & Baldwin, William (eds.), *The New Newgate Calendar*, 5 Vols. (London: J. & J. Cundee, 1825). Text available from *Ex-Classics* http://www.exclassics.com/newgate/ngintro.htm

Knapp, Robert, *Invisible Romans: Prostitutes, Outlaws, Slaves, Gladiators, Ordinary men and Women; the Romans that History Forgot* (London: Profile, 2011)

Knight, Stephen, *Robin Hood: A Mythic Biography* (Ithaca: Cornell University Press, 2003)

——, *Reading Robin Hood: Content, Form and Reception in the Outlaw Myth* (Manchester: Manchester University Press, 2015)

——, *Robin Hood: A Complete Study of the English Outlaw* (Oxford: Blackwell, 1994)

——, & Ohlgren, Thomas (eds.), *Robin Hood and Other Outlaw Tales* (Kalamazoo, MI: Medieval Institute Publications, 2000)

Langland, William, *Piers Plowman* ed. by Robertson, Elizabeth & Shepherd, Stephen H. A. (New York: Norton, 2006)

Linebaugh, Peter, *The London Hanged: Crime and Civil Society in the Eighteenth Century* (London: Penguin, 1991)

Mackie, Erin, *Rakes, Highwaymen and Pirates: The Making of the Modern Gentleman in the Eighteenth Century* (Baltimore: Johns Hopkins University Press, 2009)

Mayhew, Henry, *London Labour and the London Poor*, ed. by Robert Douglas Fairhurst (Oxford: Oxford University Press, 2010)

McConville, Sean, *A History of English Prison Administration* (Abingdon: Routledge, 1981; repr. 2013)

McKenzie, Andrea, *Tyburn's Martyrs: Execution in England, 1675-1777* (London: Continuum, 2007)

McLynn, Frank, *Crime and Punishment in Eighteenth Century England* (New York: Routledge, 1989)

Moore, Lucy, *The Thieves' Opera* (London: Penguin, 1997)

——, ed., *Conmen and Cutpurses: Scenes from the Hogarthian Underworld* (London: Penguin, 2001)

Murray, W. H., *Rob Roy Macgregor: His Life & Times* (Edinburgh: Canongate Books, 2000)

Percy, Thomas, *Reliques of Ancient English Poetry*, 3 Vols. (London: J. Dodsley, 1765). Text available from *Ex-Classics* http://www.exclassics.com/percy/percintr.htm

Pollard, A. J., *Imagining Robin Hood: The Late Medieval Stories in Historical Context* (Abingdon: Routledge, 2007)

Priestman, Martin, ed., *The Cambridge Companion to Crime Fiction* (Cambridge: Cambridge University Press, 2003)

Ohlgren, Thomas, *Robin Hood: The Early Poems, 1465-1560 - Texts, Contexts, and Ideology* (Newark, DE: University of Delaware Press, 2007)

——, ed., *Medieval Outlaws: Ten Tales in Modern English* (Stroud: Sutton, 1998)

Poe, Edgar Allen, *The Murders in the Rue Morgue and Other Tales* (London: Penguin, 2012)

Reynolds, G. W. M., *The Mysteries of London*, ed. by Trefor Thomas (London: Keele University Press, 1996)

Ritson, Joseph, ed., *Robin Hood: A Collection of All the Ancient Poems, Songs, and Ballads* 2 Vols. (London: T. Egerton, 1795). Text available from the Internet Archive https://archive.org/details/odcollectrobinho00ritsrich

Sartore, Melissa, *Outlawry, Governance, and Law in Medieval England* (New York: Peter Lang, 2013)

Scott, Walter, *Ivanhoe*, ed. by David Blair (London: Wordsworth, 1995)

——, *The Pirate*, ed. by M. Weinstein (Edinburgh: Edinburgh University Press, 2001)

——, *Rob Roy*, ed. by David Hewitt (Edinburgh: Edinburgh University Press, 2008)

Sharpe, James, *Dick Turpin: The Myth of the English Highwayman* (London: Profile Books, 2004)

Shaw, B. D., 'Bandits in the Roman Empire', *Past & Present*, No. 105 (1984), pp. 3-52

Shoemaker, Robert B., 'The Old Bailey Proceedings and the Representation of Crime and Criminal Justice in eighteenth-century London', *Journal of British Studies* 47: 3 (2008), pp. 559-580

——, 'The Street Robber and the Gentleman Highwayman: Changing Representations and Perceptions of Robbery in London, 1690-1800', *Cultural and Social History* 3: 4 (2006), pp. 381-405

——, *Prosecution and Punishment: Petty Crime and the Law in London and Rural Middlesex, c. 1660-1725* (Cambridge: Cambridge University Press, 1991)

Shore, Heather, *London's Criminal Underworlds, c. 1720-c. 1930: A Social and Cultural History* (Basingstoke: Palgrave, 2015)

——, *Artful Dodgers: Youth and Crime in Early Nineteenth-Century London* (Woodbridge: Boydell, 1999)

Smith, Alexander, *A Complete History of the Lives and Robberies of the Most Notorious Highwaymen* ed. by Heyward, Arthur (London: Routledge, 1927)

FURTHER READING

Spraggs, Gillian, *Outlaws and Highwaymen: The Cult of the Robber in England from the Middle Ages to the Nineteenth Century* (London: Pimlico, 2001)

Stevenson, David, *The Hunt For Rob Roy: The Man And The Myths* (Edinburgh: John Donald, 2004)

Tranter, Nigel, *Rob Roy MacGregor* (Castle Douglas: Neil Wilson, 2004)

Wright, Allen, 'The Search for a Real Robin Hood', *Robin Hood: Bold Outlaw of Barnsdale and Sherwood*, online edn. <<www.boldoutlaw.com/realrob/realrob2.com>> [Accessed 23 January 2018]

Notes

Preface

1   William Langland, *Piers Plowman* ed. by Elizabeth Robertson & Stephen H. A. Shepherd (New York: Norton, 2006), pp. 82-3.

2   'A Gest of Robyn Hode', in *Robin Hood: A Collection of All the Ancient Poems, Songs, and Ballads* ed. by Joseph Ritson 2 Vols. (London: T. Egerton, 1795), pp. 1-81 (p.5).

3   Dobson & Taylor, *Rymes of Robyn Hood*, p. 256; 'by no stretch of the imagination can the 'Robyn' of this lyric be properly identified with the Robin Hood of the other ballads'.

4   Thomas Ohlgren, 'A Gest of Robyn Hode', *Medieval Outlaws: Ten Tales in Modern English* ed. by Thomas Ohlgren (Stroud: Sutton, 1998), pp. 216-38.

5   Hal Gladfelder, *Criminality and Narrative in Eighteenth-Century England: Beyond the Law* (Baltimore: Johns Hopkins University Press, 2001), p. 26.

6   Michael Alpert (Trans.), *Lazarillo de Tormes and The Swindler: Two Spanish Picaresque Novels* (London: Penguin, 2003), pp. 54-5.

7   Richard Head, *The English Rogue Described in the Life of Meriton Latroon* (London: Henry Marsh, 1665), p. 16.

8   Head, *The English Rogue*, pp. 40-1

9   'An Act Concerning Outlandish People Calling Themselves Egyptians (22 Henry VIII, c. 10)', in *The Statutes at Large*, ed. by D. Pickering, 46 Vols (Cambridge: J. Bentham, 1763), 4: 205.

10 Head, *The English Rogue*, p. i.

11 Moseley, 'Richard Head's "The English Rogue"', p. 103.

12 Henry Fielding, *An Enquiry Into the Causes of the Late Increase of Robbers, &c.* (London: A. Millar, 1751), p. 2.

13 *Ibid.*, p. 116.

14 Lincoln B. Faller, *Turned to Account: The Forms and Functions of Late Seventeenth and Early Eighteenth-Century Criminal Biography* (Cambridge: Cambridge University Press, 1987), p. x.

15 Daniel Defoe, cited in P. N. Furbank & W. R. Owens, *Defoe De-Attributions: A Critique of J.R. Moore's Checklist* (London: Hambledon, 1994), p. 1.

16 Stephen Basdeo, 'Robin Hood the Brute: Representations of the Outlaw in 18th-Century Criminal Biography', *Law, Crime, and History*, 6: 2 (2016), pp. 54-70 (p. 69n).

Chapter 1

17 Alexander Kaufman, 'Histories of Contexts: Form, Argument, and Ideology in *A Gest of Robyn Hode*', in *British Outlaws of Literature and History: Essays on Medieval and Early Modern Figures from Robin Hood to Twm Shon Catty* ed. by Alexander Kaufman (Jefferson, NC: MacFarland, 2011), pp. 146-164 (p. 146).

18 'A Gest of Robyn Hode', p. 90.

19 *Ibid.*, p. 80.

20 'Robin Hood and Guy of Gisborne', p. 178.

21 'Robin Hood and the Monk', p. 43.

22 Ritson, *Robin Hood,* 1: iv.

23 Ritson, *Robin Hood*, 1: xii.

24 Ritson, *Robin Hood*, 1: v

25 Ritson, *Robin Hood*, 1: ix.

26 Walter Scott, *Ivanhoe* (London: MacMillan, 1910), p. 3.

27 W. E. Simeone, 'The Robin Hood of Ivanhoe', *The Journal of American Folklore* 74: 293 (1961), pp. 230-234 (p. 231).

28 Thomas Love Peacock, *Maid Marian and Crochet Castle*, ed. by G. Saintsbury (London: MacMillan, 1895), p. 126.

29 Peacock, *Maid Marian*, p. 84.

30 Knight, *Robin Hood: A Mythic Biography*, p. 153.

31 *Ibid.*, p. 152.

Chapter 2

32 'Adam Bell, Clim of the Clough, and William of Cloudeslie', in *A Lytell Geste of Robin Hode* ed. by John Mathew Gutch 2 Vols. (London: Longman, 1847), 2: 320.

33 'Robin Hood and the Potter', in *Robin Hood: A Collection of all the Ancient Poems, Songs, and Ballads* ed. by Joseph Ritson 2 Vols. (London: T. Egerton, 1795), 1: 82.

34 'Adam Bell, Clim of the Clough, and William of Cloudeslie', 2: 325.

35 *Ibid.*, 2: 329.

36 *Ibid.*, 2: 332.

37 *Ibid.*, 2: 337.

38 *Ibid.*, 2: 339.

39 *Ibid.*, 2: 342.

40 Pierce Egan, *Adam Bell, Clim of the Clough, and William of Cloudesley* (London: G. Pierce [n. d.]), pp. 1-2.

Chapter 3

41 *The Life and Death of Gamaliel Ratsey, a Famous Theefe of England, Executed at Bedford the 26 of March Last Past, 1605* (London: V. Simmes, 1605), [p. 4]. The surviving copy of this publication is not paginated, and references to page numbers are my own insertion.

42 *Ibid.*, [p. 14].

43 John Awdley, *The Fraternity of Vacabondes* (London, 1561; repr. London: J. Awdley, 1575), [p. 4]. Early editions of this work are not paginated, but I have inserted page numbers for ease of reference.

44 *Ibid.*, [pp. 4-5].

45 *Ibid.*, [p. 4].

46 *The Life and Death of Gamaliel Ratsey*, [p. 16].

Chapter 4

47 Alexander Smith, *A Complete History of the Lives and Robberies of the Most Notorious Highwaymen*, ed. by Arthur Heyward (London: Routledge, 1927), p. 138.

48 Information for this account of the life of James Hind is taken from several contemporary accounts printed shortly after his death: *The English Gusman; or, The History of that Unparallel'd Thief, James Hind* (London: Printed by T. N. for George Latham Junior, 1652); *No Jest like a True Iest, being a Compendious Record of the Merry Life and Mad Exploits of Captain James Hind, the Great Robber of England. Together with the Close of all a Worcestor, where he was*

Hang'd and Quarter'd for High Treason Against the Commonwealth
(London: T. Vere, 1652); *The Pleasant and Delightful History
of Captain Hind* (London: George Horton, 1651); *A Second and
Discovery of Hind's Exploits: or, A Fuller Relation of his Ramble,
Robberies and Cheats in England, Ireland, and Scotland, with
his Voyage to Holland* (London: William Ley, 1652). Only direct
quotations will be referenced from hereon.

49   *The English Gusman*, p. 2.

50   *Ibid.*

51   Charles Johnson, *Lives of the Most Remarkable Criminals* ed. by
Arthur Heyward (London: Routledge, 1927), p. 211

52   *The Guardian.* 2 Vols (London: Longman, 1801), 1: 267.

53   Joseph Ritson, *An Essay on Abstinence from Animal Food as a Moral
Duty* (London: Richard Phillips, 1802), p. 229.

54   Richard Head, *The English Rogue Described in the Life of Meriton
Latroon* (London: H. Marsh, 1665), pp. 16-17

55   *The English Gusman*, p. 4.

56   *Ibid.*

57   Alexander Smith, *A Compleat History of the Lives and Robberies of
the Most Notorious Highway-men, Foot-pads, Shop-lifts, and Cheats,
of both Sexes*, 3 vols. (London: J. Morphew, 1719), 1: 137.

58   *The English Gusman*, p. 38.

59   *An Account of the Whole Proceedings at the Sessions* ([n. p.]:
[n. pub.], 1683), p. 2.

60   *The English Gusman*, p. 40.

61   *Captain Hind's Progress and Ramble* ([n. p.], [n. pub.], [n. d.]).

Chapter 5

62   *A Compleat Collection of Remarkable Tryals of the Most Notorious
Malefactors, at the Sessions-House in the Old Baily, for Near Fifty
Years' Past*, 4 Vols (London: J. Phillips, 1718), 1: 42.

63   'Claude Du Vall', *The Newgate Calendar*
[Internet <http://www.exclassics.com/newgate/ng31.htm>].

64   Walter Pope, *The Memoires of Monsieur Du Vall: Containing the
History of his Life and Death Whereunto are Annexed His last Speech
and Epitaph* (London: H. Brome, 1670), pp. 14-15.

65   Smith, *Highwaymen*, p. 148.

66   *Ibid.*, p. 148.

Chapter 6

67 Lincoln B. Faller, *Turned to Account: The Forms and Functions of Criminal Biography in Late Seventeenth- and Early Eighteenth-Century England* (Cambridge: Cambridge University Press, 1987), p. 127.

68 Johnson, *Highwaymen*, p. 26.

69 *Ibid.*, p. 26.

70 Thomas Beard & Thomas Taylor, *The Theatre of God's Judgements: Wherein is Represented the Admirable Iustice of God Against All Notorious Sinners, Great and Small, Specially Against the Most Eminent Persons in the World, Whose Exorbitant Power Had Broke through the Barres of Divine and Human Law. Collected out of Sacred, Ecclesiastical, and Pagan Histories by Two Most Reverend Doctors in Divinity, Thomas Beard of Huntington and Taylor, the Famous Late Preacher of Mary Aldermanbury in London. The Incomparable Use of this Book for Ministers and Others is Largely Expressed in the Preface. The Fourth Edition, with Editions* (London, 1597; repr. London: Printed by S. I. & M. H. and are to be sold by Richard Whitaker at the Signe of the Kings Armes in St. Pauls Churchyard, 1648), p. 214.

71 John Fielding, *True Examples of the Interposition of Divine Providence in the Discovery and Punishment of Murder* (London: J. Marshall, [n. d.]), p. 2.

72 Johnson, *Highwaymen*, p. 28.

73 *Ibid.*

74 *Ibid.*, p. 129.

Chapter 7

75 *The Highland Rogue: or, The Memorable Actions of the Celebrated Robert Mac-Gregor, Commonly Called Rob Roy* (London: J. Billingsley, 1723), p. x.

76 *The Highland Rogue.*, p. xi.

77 *Ibid.*, p. 16.

78 *Ibid.*, p. 19.

79 Walter Scott, *Rob Roy, with the Author's Last Notes and Additions* (Paris: Baudry's Foreign Library, 1831), p. xx-i.

80 *The Highland Rogue*, p. 36.

81   Bosley Crowther, 'Rob Roy Opens at Criterion', *New York Times*, 4 February 1954 [Internet <http://www.nytimes.com> Accessed 21 January 2018].

Chapter 8

82   This account of Jack Sheppard's life is taken largely from the following sources: *Authentic Memoirs of the Life and Surprising Adventures of John Sheppard: Who was Executed at Tyburn, November the 16th, 1724. By Way of Familiar Letters from a Gentleman in Town, to his Friend and Correspondent in the Country* 2nd Edn. (London: Joseph Merchant, 1724); *The History of the Remarkable Life of John Sheppard* (London: John Applebee, 1724); *A Narrative of all the Robberies, Escapes, &c. of John Sheppard* (London: Printed and Sold by John Applebee, 1724).

83   *The History of the Remarkable Life of John Sheppard*, p. 2.

84   *Ibid*.

85   John Gay, *The Beggar's Opera* 3rd Edn. (London: J. Watts, 1729), p. 28.

86   *The Proceedings on the King's Commission of the Peace, and Oyer and Terminer, and Gaol-Delivery of Newgate, held for the City of London and County of Middlesex, at Justice Hall in the Old Bailey, on Wednesday 8th, 9th, and 10th of July, in the Tenth Year of his Majesty's Reign* (London: Printed for J. Humphreys, 1724), p. 6.

87   *Ibid*, p. 31.

88   'Review', *The Athenaeum* 26 October 1840, pp. 803-05.

89   Ainsworth, 'To the Editor of The Times', p. 7.

90   Samuel Phillips Day, *Juvenile Crime: Its Causes, Character, and Cure* (London: J. F. Hope, 1858), cited in Robert J. Kirkpatrick, *Children's Books History Society Occasional Paper XI: Wild Boys in the Dock – Victorian Juvenile Literature and Juvenile Crime* (London: Children's Books History Society, 2013), p. 21.

91   Henry Mayhew & John Binny, *The Criminal Prisons of London and Scenes of Prison Life* (London: Griffin, 1862), p. 45.

92   *Edinburgh Evening News* 6 July 1876, cited in Kirkpatrick, *Wild Boys in the Dock*, p. 10.

93   G. K. Chesterton, *The Wayfarer's Library: The Defendant* (London: J. M. Dent, 1901) [Internet <http://www.gkc.org.uk/gkc/books/penny-dreadfuls.html>.

Chapter 9

94 'Advertistment', *Daily Courant* 22 November 1715, p. 2.
95 Gay, *The Beggar's Opera*, pp. 2-3.
96 *The True and Genuine Account of the Life and Actions of the Life and Actions of the Late Jonathan Wild*, p. 20.
97 Camden Pelham, *The Chronicles of Crime; or, The New Newgate Calendar* (London, 1840; repr. London: T. Miles, 1881), p. 59.
98 Alexander Smith, *The Comical and Tragical History of the Lives and Adventures of the Most Bayliffs* (London: Samuel Briscoe, 1723), p. 20.
99 *Ibid.*, pp. 41-50.
100 Henry Fielding, *The History of the Life of Mr. Jonathan Wild the Great* (London, 1743; repr. London: J. Bell, 1775), p. 3.
101 *Ibid.*, p. 3.
102 *Ibid.*, p. 32.
103 *Ibid.*, pp. 49-50.
104 *Ibid.*, pp. 195-6.

Chapter 10

105 *The Genuine History of the Life of Richard Turpin, the Noted Highwayman, Who was Executed at York for Horse-Stealing, under the Name of John Palmer, on Saturday Ap. 7, 1739* (London: Printed for J. Standen, at D'Anver's Head opposite Serjeants-Inn in Chancery Lane, 1739), p. 1
106 *The Genuine History of the Life of Richard Turpin*, p. 3.
107 Richard Steele & Joseph Addison, *The Tatler; or, The Lucubrations of Isaac Bickerstaffe*, 4 Vols. (London: C. Bathurst, 1774), 2: 188.
108 *The Genuine History of the Life of Richard Turpin, the Noted Highwayman*, p. 15.
109 *Ibid.*, p. 21.
110 *Ibid.*, p. 21.
111 *Ibid.*
112 *The Trial of the Notorious Highwayman, Richard Turpin* (York: Ward & Chandler, 1739), pp. 21-22.
113 William Harrison Ainsworth, *Rookwood: A Romance* (London: Chapman and Hall, 1930), p.157.

114 *Ibid.*, p. 340.

115 *Ibid.*, p. 202.

116 *Ibid.*, p. 54.

117 *Turpin's Ride to York* (Manchester: J. Cadman, c. 1840)

Chapter 11

118 Johnson, *Remarkable Criminals*, p. 9.

119 William Dodd, *Thoughts in Prison; in Five Parts, viz., the Imprisonment, the Retrospect, Public Punishment, the Trial, Futurity* (London: T. Miller, 1815), p. i.

120 *The Newgate Calendar; Comprising Interesting Memoirs of the Most Notorious Characters who have been Convicted of Outrages upon the Laws of England since the Commencement of the Eighteenth Century*, ed. by Andrew Knapp & William Baldwin, 4 Vols. (London: J. Robins, 1824-28), 3: 50.

121 Dodd, *Thoughts in Prison*, p. x.

122 Knapp and Bawldwin, *The Newgate Calendar*, p. 56.

123 *Ibid.*, p. 56.

124 *Ibid.*, p. 57.

125 Dodd, *Thoughts in Prison*, pp. 207-08.

126 Samuel Johnson, 'Letter to James Boswell' in *Boswell's Life of Johnson*, ed. by G. B. N. Hill & L. F. Powell, 6 Vols. (Oxford: Oxford University Press, 1934-64), 3:136-39.

Conclusion

127 Charles MacFarlane, *The Lives and Exploits of the Banditti and Robbers of all Nations* 2 Vols. (London, 1833 repr. London: R. W. Pomeroy, 1836), 1: 16.

128 Charles Macfarlane, *Lives and Exploits of the Most Celebrated Banditti and Robbers of all Nations* (Philadelphia: G. Evans, 1833), p. 10.

129 *Ibid.*, p. 10.

130 *Ibid.*, p. 17.

131 *Ibid.*, p. 10.

132 *The Times*, 3 October 1798, p.1

133 Report of the Capital Punishment Commission (London: George E. Eyre, 1866), p. 240.

134 Anon. 'Great Expectations', *The Times* 17 October 1861, p. 6

135 Charlotte M. Yonge, *What Books to Lend and What to Give* (London: [n.p. n.d.]), pp. 5-6.

136 Andrew Mearns, 'The Bitter Cry of Outcast London (1883)', *WTSRS: W. T. Stead Resource Site*, ed. by Owen Mulpetre, online edn. https://attackingthedevil.co.uk/related/outcast.php.

137 Gay, *The Beggar's Opera*, p. 57.

Appendix

138 Judges 9: 25. *New English Translation.*

139 Ezra 8: 31. *New English Translation.*

140 Luke 10: 30. *New International Version.*

141 Matthew 27: 38; Mark 15: 27. *New American Standard Bible.*

142 Herodian, *The History of the Roman Empire* Trans. E. C. Echols (Los Angeles: University of California Press, 1961) [Internet <http://www.tertullian.org/fathers/herodian_01_book1.htm>.

143 Cassius Dio, *The Loeb Classical Library: Roman History* Trans. Earnest Cary 9 Vols. (Cambridge, MA: Harvard University Press, 1927), 9: 260

144 Dio, *The Loeb Classical Library: Roman History*, 9: 259.

145 Dio, *The Loeb Classical Library: Roman History*, 9: 260

146 Shaw, 'Bandits in the Roman Empire', p. 14.

147 Shaw, 'Bandits in the Roman Empire', p. 16; a *receptatore* could also mean a 'fence'.

Index